Encyclopedia of the Animal World

Fish

Jill Bailey

Facts On File

New York • Oxford

FISH
The Encyclopedia of the Animal World

Managing Editor: Lionel Bender
Art Editor: Ben White
Designer: Malcolm Smythe
Text Editor: Madeleine Samuel
Project Editor: Graham Bateman
Production: Clive Sparling, Joanna
    Turner

Media conversion and typesetting:
    Robert and Peter MacDonald,
    Una Macnamara

AN EQUINOX BOOK

Planned and produced by:
Equinox (Oxford) Limited,
Musterlin House, Jordan Hill Road,
Oxford OX2 8DP

Prepared by Lionheart Books

British Library Cataloguing in
Publication Data
Bailey, Jill
    Fish
    (Encyclopedia of the Animal World)
    1. Marine and freshwater fish
    I. Title   II. Series
    591.92

ISBN 0-8160-1966-5

Published in Great Britain by
Facts On File Limited, Collins Street
Oxford, England OX4 1XJ

Origination by Alpha Reprographics Ltd,
Perivale, Middx, England

Printed in Italy.

10 9 8 7 6 5 4 3 2 1

FACT PANEL: Key to symbols denoting general features of animals

SYMBOLS WITH NO WORDS

Group size

■ Solitary

■ Small groups (up to 10)

■ Large groups (shoals)

◩ Variable

Conservation status

☠ All species threatened

✗ Some species threatened

No species threatened (no
symbol)

SYMBOLS NEXT TO HEADINGS

Habitat

▨ Sea

◉ Fresh water

▨ Fresh and/or Sea water

Diet

■ Other animals

■ Plants

◩ Animals and Plants

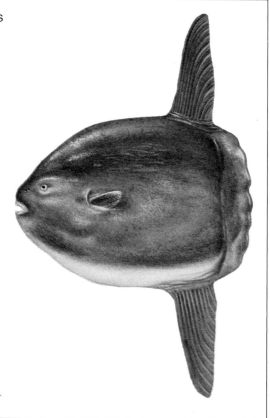

CONTENTS

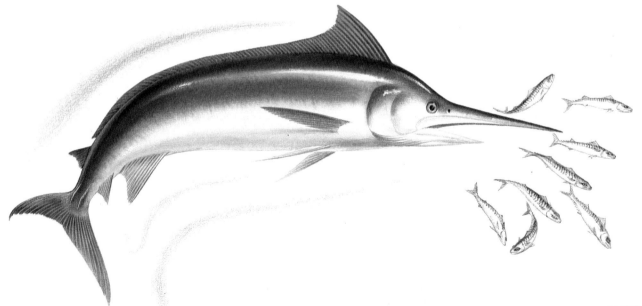

INTRODUCTION

The *Encyclopedia of the Animal World* surveys the main groups and species of animals alive today. Written by a team of specialists, it includes the most current information and the newest ideas on animal behaviour and survival. The Encyclopedia looks at how the shape and form of an animal reflect its life-style – the ways in which a creature's size, colour, feeding methods and defences have all evolved in relationship to a particular diet, climate and habitat. Discussed also are the ways in which human activities often disrupt natural ecosystems and threaten the survival of many species.

In this Encyclopedia the animals are grouped on the basis of their body structure and their evolution from common ancestors. Thus, there are single volumes or groups of volumes on mammals, birds, reptiles and amphibians, fish, insects and so on. Within these major categories, the animals are grouped according to their feeding habits or general life-styles. Because there is so much information on the animals in two of these major categories, there are four volumes devoted to mammals (*The Small Plant-Eaters; The Hunters; The Large Plant-Eaters; Primates, Insect-Eaters and Baleen Whales*) and three to birds (*The Waterbirds; The Aerial Hunters; The Plant- and Seed-Eaters*).

This volume, *Fish*, includes entries on lampreys, sharks, sturgeons, garfish, eels, herrings, pike, salmon, lantern fish, carp, catfish, cod, killifish, perch, lungfish and the coelacanth. Together they number about 21,000 species. Fish are all vertebrates – they have a skull that surrounds a well-developed brain, and a spinal column of cartilage or bone. They are also totally aquatic; with a few exceptions such as lungfish and some eels, they do not come out of water on to land.

Fish are found in almost every watery habitat, from the cold dark waters of the deepest oceans to lakes high in the Andes mountains, in mud and underground. They do almost everything that other vertebrates (amphibians, reptiles, birds, mammals) do, and many things they do not. An Amazonian species of guppy comprises only females. There are luminous fish, transparent fish and electric fish. Their size range is colossal, from tropical freshwater species only a few centimetres long, to sharks up to 12m in length and weighing 12 tonnes. Cod, whiting, plaice, anchovy and tunas number countless millions of individuals, while the coelacanth just manages to survive with perhaps only a few hundred.

To some people, the typical fish is the sharp-toothed shark, elegantly and effortlessly hunting its prey in the sea.

To others it is the salmon or trout they are about to eat from a dinner plate, or the small pretty animals that fill an aquarium at home or in a zoo. For anglers, fish are a cunning quarry to be outwitted and caught. To biologists – the scientists who study living things – fish are a link between "simple animals", such as starfish and lobsters, and higher vertebrates, which include mammals such as ourselves.

Each article in this Encyclopedia is devoted to an individual species or group of closely related species. The text starts with a short scene-setting story that highlights one or more of the animal's unique features. It then continues with details of the most interesting aspects of the animal's physical features and abilities, diet and feeding behaviour, and general life-style. It also covers conservation and the animal's relationships with people.

A fact panel provides easy reference to the main features of distribution (natural, not introductions to other areas by humans), habitat, diet, size, colour and breeding. (An explanation of the colour-coded symbols is given on page 2 of the book.) The panel also includes a list of the common and scientific (Latin) names of species mentioned in the main text and photo captions. For species illustrated in major artwork panels but not described elsewhere, the names are given in the caption accompanying the artwork. In such illustrations, animals are shown to scale unless otherwise stated; actual dimensions may be found in the text. To help the reader quickly determine the type of animal each article deals with, in the upper right part of the page at the beginning of an article is a simple line drawing of one or more representative species.

Many species of animal are threatened with extinction as a result of human activities. In this Encyclopedia the following terms are used to show the status of a species as defined by the International Union for the Conservation of Nature and Natural Resources:

Endangered – in danger of extinction unless their habitat is no longer destroyed and they are not hunted by people.

Vulnerable – likely to become endangered in the near future.

Rare – exist in small numbers but neither endangered nor vulnerable at present.

A glossary provides definitions of technical terms used in the book. A common name and scientific (Latin) name index provide easy access to text and illustrations.

Photo opposite: These Potato cod are food for larger predatory fish like sharks.

WHAT IS A FISH?

Fish are all cold-blooded vertebrates (animals with backbones) without any legs, which live in fresh- or sea-water. Their blood is not necessarily cold – the blood of fish living in tropical seas may be warmer than ours (37°C) – but they are unable to produce internal heat as mammals and birds can. Thus, their body temperature is reliant upon the warmth of their surroundings. Scientists usually prefer to call such animals ectothermic rather than cold-blooded, from the Greek *ekto* outside and *therme* heat.

Most fish breathe by means of gills, obtaining oxygen from the water and not from the air. Their shape is usually streamlined: there is no obvious neck, and the body simply tapers smoothly towards the head and tail. Many fish are covered in scales, and most have fins to help them swim.

►The first fish appeared on Earth about 500 million years ago. These armour-plated fish gradually evolved over time jaws, paired fins, bony or cartilaginous skeletons, and light, flexible scales instead of bony plates, to produce all the shapes and sizes of fish we know today.

▼The Congo tetra, a typical bony fish with fins bearing supporting rays.

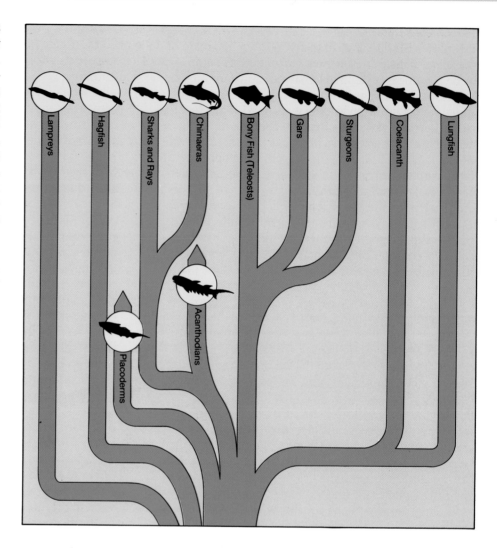

Lampreys
Hagfish
Sharks and Rays
Chimaeras
Bony Fish (Teleosts)
Gars
Sturgeons
Coelacanth
Lungfish
Acanthodians
Placoderms

TYPES OF FISH

The word fish does not have any real meaning in fish classification. While birds and mammals comprise distinct groups, or classes, of vertebrates, the animals we call fish belong to four very different classes of animals which just happen to look similar.

The Bony Fish

The most important class today is the Osteichthyes, with more than 20,000 species. Most bony fish are covered in flat scales, and their gills are protected by a distinct plate, the operculum. Their skeleton is made of bone.

The Cartilaginous Fish

The sharks, skates and rays belong to the class Chondrichthyes, which has over 700 species. Their bodies are covered in rough scales. Their gills open to the outside through a series of long slits; there is no operculum. The skeleton is composed of cartilage, a much softer and more flexible type of tissue than bone.

The Jawless Fish

The lampreys, class Cephalaspidomorphi (about 40 species), and the hagfish, class Myxini (32 species), have no jaws, no true teeth and no paired fins like those of the cartilaginous and bony fish. Their gills open directly to the outside through a series of

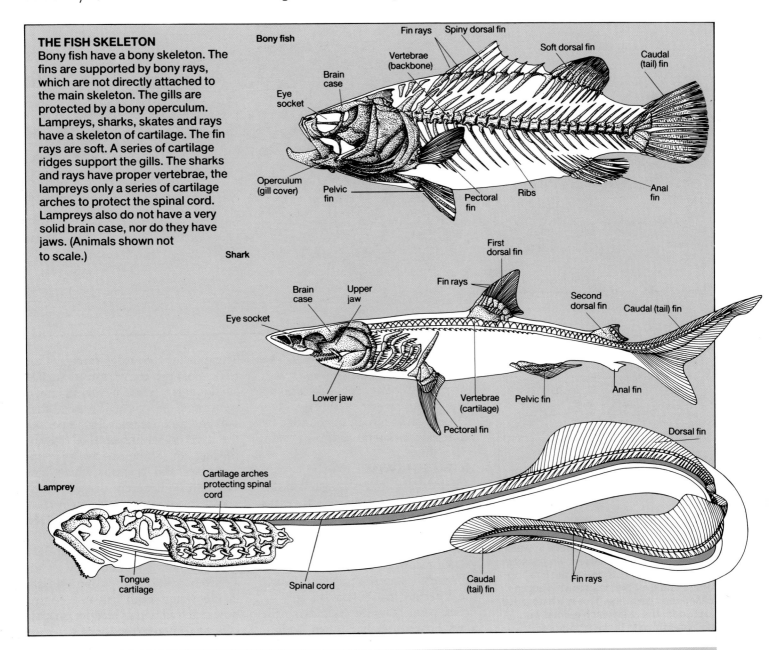

THE FISH SKELETON
Bony fish have a bony skeleton. The fins are supported by bony rays, which are not directly attached to the main skeleton. The gills are protected by a bony operculum. Lampreys, sharks, skates and rays have a skeleton of cartilage. The fin rays are soft. A series of cartilage ridges support the gills. The sharks and rays have proper vertebrae, the lampreys only a series of cartilage arches to protect the spinal cord. Lampreys also do not have a very solid brain case, nor do they have jaws. (Animals shown not to scale.)

Bony fish

Fin rays   Spiny dorsal fin   Soft dorsal fin   Caudal (tail) fin
Vertebrae (backbone)
Brain case
Eye socket
Operculum (gill cover)   Pelvic fin   Pectoral fin   Ribs   Anal fin

Shark

First dorsal fin
Fin rays
Brain case   Upper jaw   Second dorsal fin   Caudal (tail) fin
Eye socket
Lower jaw   Vertebrae (cartilage)   Pelvic fin   Anal fin
Pectoral fin

Lamprey

Cartilage arches protecting spinal cord
Dorsal fin
Tongue cartilage   Spinal cord   Caudal (tail) fin   Fin rays

▶Fish scales viewed under a microscope show beautiful colours. Scales overlap to form a protective covering over the fish. They are bony plates made in the skin. In most fish they remain covered by very thin skin, but in sharks, skates and rays the scales grow out through their skin. Each scale has a series of tiny ring-shaped ridges.

▼Fins have many different uses. The dorsal and ventral fins help to prevent the fish from rolling or slewing sideways. The fish can use its paired pectoral and pelvic fins to control its angle in the water, so it can swim up or down. These fins are also used as brakes. The tail fin is used as a rudder for steering. It is usually very broad.

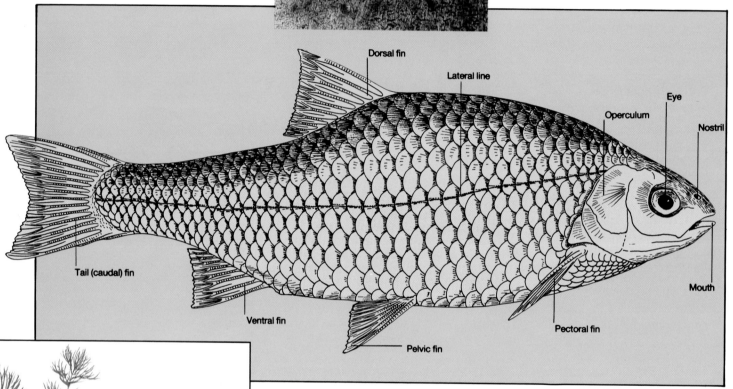

Dorsal fin

Lateral line

Eye

Operculum

Nostril

Tail (caudal) fin

Mouth

Ventral fin

Pectoral fin

Pelvic fin

▲Fish can detect the vibrations in water caused by other animals moving nearby. Running along each side of the fish and branching over the head is a silvery line called the lateral line. This is a long canal just under the skin which is lined with cells sensitive to these vibrations.

small round holes, or spiracles. The lamprey mouth is a large sucker with horny teeth. The hagfish have no skeleton, no proper eyes, several sets of hearts, and a mouth surrounded by numerous thick tentacles.

HOW FISH SWIM

Most fish have bodies designed to slip through the water easily – they are very streamlined. They are mostly torpedo-shaped, tapering at the head and tail. Glands in the fish's skin produce slimy mucus which helps to lubricate the animal's passage through the water as it moves forward.

Fish propel themselves in two main ways. Firstly, they bend their bodies.

This pushes the water sideways and back, so they move forwards. Fish such as eels rely heavily on this kind of swimming. Secondly, fish bend their tails and also use their fins, especially the large dorsal fins on the back and the tail fin. Some species, like the seahorses and boxfish, which have very stiff bodies, rely almost entirely on their pectoral fins to scull them along. Fish use their paired fins also for steering and braking.

Most bony fish have an air-filled swimbladder. The buoyancy of the air, like a balloon, stops them sinking in the water. Each fish can control how much air is in its bladder, so it can adjust to different depths of water.

Sharks, skates and rays do not have swimbladders. Like a plane in the air, they must move forward to lift their bodies in the water. If they stop swimming, they sink. Some fish can reach very high speeds. A sailfish swimming near the coast of Florida was timed at 109kph, which means it took just 1 second to travel 30m.

SEEING UNDER WATER

Most fish have large bulging eyes at the sides of their heads. Because the eyes protrude, they have good all-round vision. Fish have no eyelids – they have to sleep with their eyes open. Most bony fish and lampreys can see in colour, but sharks and rays cannot. Some fish appear to see well out of water. Trout will leap out of the water and catch passing mayflies. Fish living in deep water often have very large eyes, but those living in the total darkness of the deep ocean or in caves often have very small eyes, or may even be blind. They rely on other senses to find their food.

WATER MUSIC

Sound travels five times slower in water than in air. But fish have internal ears near the back of the head, and can hear well, although not so well as we can. Sharks have been shown to hear the sound of a struggling fish from a distance of 200m.

HOW FISH BREATHE

Fish extract oxygen from the water and use it to burn up their food to produce energy for growth and movement. Instead of lungs, a fish has gills, which are little fleshy outgrowths just like rows of tiny fingers, supported by bony arches. Gills provide a huge surface area for absorbing oxygen.

▶ Mudskippers spend a lot of time out of water, using air and water trapped in their gill chambers. Their pectoral fins are like stubby little legs, and their pelvic fins form a sucker for clinging to mangrove roots. To prevent their eyes drying out, they frequently roll them back into the moist eye sockets.

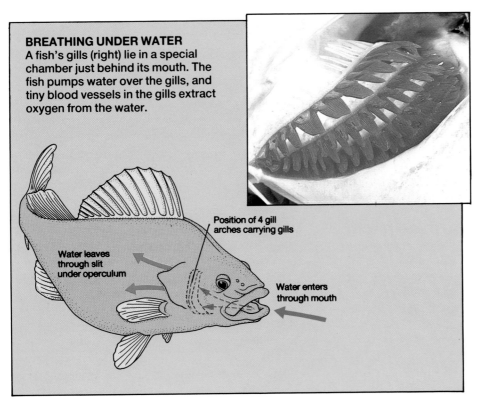

BREATHING UNDER WATER
A fish's gills (right) lie in a special chamber just behind its mouth. The fish pumps water over the gills, and tiny blood vessels in the gills extract oxygen from the water.

Position of 4 gill arches carrying gills

Water leaves through slit under operculum

Water enters through mouth

◀A female (above) and a male swordtail. This species gives birth to live young and is a popular aquarium fish.

FISH FACTS
Smallest Dwarf goby (*Pandaka pygmaea*), length 8mm.
Largest Whale shark (*Rhincodon typus*), length 12.5m.
Fastest Sailfish (*Istiophorus platypterus*), 109kph.
Commonest Deep-sea bristlemouth (*Cyclothone elongata*)
Most eggs Oceanic sunfish (*Mola mola*) 250 million+.
Lifespan Shortest: killifish (Cyprinodontidae) of desert pools, 8 months.
Longest Lake sturgeon (*Acipenser fulvescens*), over 80 years.

The fish draws water towards the gill chamber by opening its mouth and closing its gill cover. It then closes its mouth and raises the floor of the mouth. This forces the water over its gills and out through a slit under the gill cover. If you watch a fish, you can see its throat and operculum moving as it pumps water over its gills.

FROM EELS TO FLOUNDERS

The smallest fish in the world, the Dwarf goby, is less than 1cm long, while the largest, the Whale shark, may be over 12.5m long. Eels are long and thin, well suited to living in the mud and wriggling in and out of weeds. Flatfish, skates and rays are broad and flat, and spend much of their time just lying on the seabed. Butterflyfish are tall and thin, and can glide into cracks in the coral reefs in search of food. When viewed from the front, they are so narrow as to be almost invisible to predators.

Fast-swimming fish like tunas and sharks are the most torpedo-shaped. Sea horses, which are poor swimmers, swim in an upright position, and have long tails that they can curl

▶Fish come in many different shapes and sizes that suit their many life-styles.

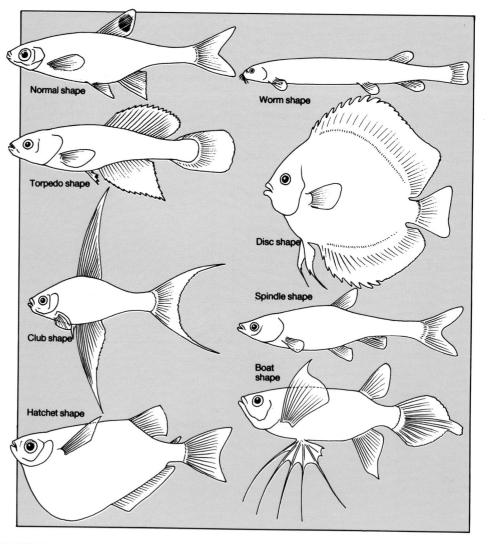

Normal shape

Worm shape

Torpedo shape

Disc shape

Club shape

Spindle shape

Boat shape

Hatchet shape

◀Blind characins from the underwater caves of Mexico. During millions of years of evolution, these fish, living in permanent darkness, have lost the power of sight.

use sound waves. The pulses bounce back like echoes from nearby objects, including moving prey. How quickly the pulses return tells the fish how far away an object is.

FROM EGG TO ADULT
Most fish mate and lay their eggs in the water. The eggs may contain oil droplets to help them float, or they may all sink to the bottom. Trout, which spawn (lay eggs) in fast-flowing rivers, make a hollow in the river bed, lay their eggs in it, then cover them with stones to prevent them being washed away. Some species, such as sticklebacks, build nests of weed for their eggs. Others, like anemone fish, glue them to rocks. A newly hatched fish often looks different from its parents, and is called a larva or fry.

Most fish lay their eggs and leave, but a few stay to guard their offspring. It is usually the male that takes care of the eggs. Mouth-brooder cichlids keep their eggs and young in their mouths for safety.

Not all fish lay eggs. Swordtails, guppies, and some sharks give birth to fully formed young. Some sharks and dogfish lay their eggs in a tough protective purse firmly anchored to seaweeds. The eggs hatch inside the purse, and the young escape as soon as they are big enough to fend for themselves.

FISH DEFENCES
Fish have many ways of defending themselves. Some, like the plaice, match their background so well that their enemies do not notice them. Others have armour-plated bodies or sharp spines. Pufferfish can inflate their bodies so they become impossible to swallow. Some fish are covered in bad-tasting or poisonous slime.

around weeds or rocks to anchor themselves. Stingrays have long thin tails with sharp spines, while ocean sunfish appear to have no tail at all.

VARIED DIETS
Fish feed on just about everything. Some, such as the White shark, are fierce predators. Sharks can twist and turn quickly to catch their prey, seizing it with their sharp teeth. Wrasses and breams can shoot their mouth forward like a funnel as soon as prey comes within reach. Anglerfish and stone fish have huge mouths, which they open suddenly, sucking in their prey. Rays and skates also rely on ambush, burying themselves in the mud with only their eyes showing. Parrotfish have a hard horny beak for scraping at corals.

Many fish, such as herrings, feed on plankton, the tiny floating plants and animals. They are filter-feeders, swimming along with their mouths open,

trapping their food on special sieves on the gills, the gill-rakers. Gill-rakers are also used by fish like the mullet, which feeds on the debris in the mud at the bottom of seas and rivers.

A few fish, such as the Grass carp and tilapia, feed on water plants. Fish teeth are not confined to the jaws. Many plant-eaters have teeth in the throat, which are used to grind up plant material.

FINDING FOOD
As well as their eyes, most fish use their powerful sense of smell and taste to find their food, detecting chemicals dissolved in the water. In muddy water, touch may be more important: some species have tentacles (barbels) around the mouth for feeling their way. Barbels are also used for tasting. Other species use electricity to find prey in murky water. Electric eels and electric catfish generate pulses of electricity and use them rather like bats

LAMPREYS, HAGFISH

The shallow water is awash with a writhing mass of silvery bodies as the Sea lampreys make their way upstream to spawn. From time to time a pair of them separates from the rest to excavate a nest hollow in the stony river bed, using their suckers to move the stones. Twined round each other, they mate and shed their eggs. Exhausted by the long journey from the ocean and the effort of spawning, they will soon die.

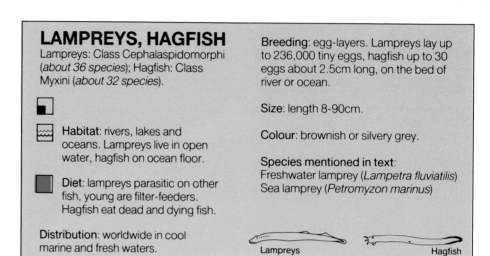

LAMPREYS, HAGFISH
Lampreys: Class Cephalaspidomorphi (*about 36 species*); Hagfish: Class Myxini (*about 32 species*).

■◪

Habitat: rivers, lakes and oceans. Lampreys live in open water, hagfish on ocean floor.

Diet: lampreys parasitic on other fish, young are filter-feeders. Hagfish eat dead and dying fish.

Distribution: worldwide in cool marine and fresh waters.

Breeding: egg-layers. Lampreys lay up to 236,000 tiny eggs, hagfish up to 30 eggs about 2.5cm long, on the bed of river or ocean.

Size: length 8-90cm.

Colour: brownish or silvery grey.

Species mentioned in text:
Freshwater lamprey (*Lampetra fluviatilis*)
Sea lamprey (*Petromyzon marinus*)

Lampreys   Hagfish

Lampreys and hagfish are primitive fish that do not have jaws and look much like eels. They have no proper skull, and their skeletons are made of cartilage, not bone. The skin is tough and exceedingly slimy, with no scales. The slime acts as a kind of protection as it makes them difficult to grip and unpleasant or harmful to eat. The single nostril opens into the throat, and the gills open to the outside through a series of small holes or spiracles behind the eyes.

PRIMITIVE PARASITES
Lampreys have fins along their backs as well as on their tails, but they have no paired fins. There are seven pairs of gills, and seven spiracles. The mouth is like a large sucker, armed with circular rows of horny teeth. On the top of the head, between the eyes, is a special organ just under the skin which is sensitive to light and dark.

Most adult lampreys are parasites of other fish species, for example trout. They can cause great damage to commercially important fish stocks. The lamprey clings to the side of its host with its sucker, then uses its horny teeth to cut through the victim's skin and scales. It feeds on the host's blood, injecting a chemical to prevent the blood clotting. A few species do not feed at all as adults.

AMAZING TRANSFORMATION
The young fish that hatches from a lamprey's egg looks like a small worm, and is called an ammocoete larva. It lives in the mud with only its head showing. Its toothless mouth is ringed with fleshy filaments covered in sticky mucus which trap particles of food from the water.

After 3 to 7 years, the ammocoete stops feeding for several months and undergoes a dramatic change. The eyes develop, and the mouth soon becomes sucker-like and develops a rasping tongue and horny teeth. At first the young lamprey preys on small fish and invertebrates. Once it is big enough to start life as a parasite, it travels far. Adult Freshwater lampreys travel downstream. Adult Sea lampreys reach the sea, and may travel many kilometres before returning to the river many years later to spawn.

▼▶ **Species of lamprey and hagfish**
Juvenile Freshwater lampreys (ammocoete larvae) **(1)** filter food from the water. A Sea lamprey **(2)** builds a nest. Brook lampreys (*Lampetra planeri*) **(3)** feed on a trout. A hagfish, *Myxine* species, **(4)** ties itself in a knot as it burrows into its prey. An adult hagfish **(5)** looks like an adult eel.

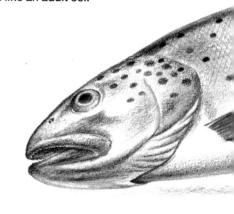

1

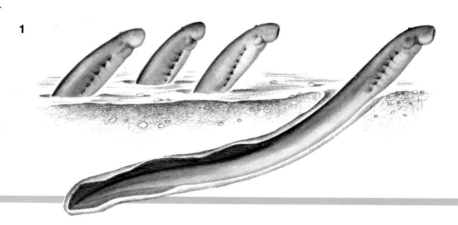

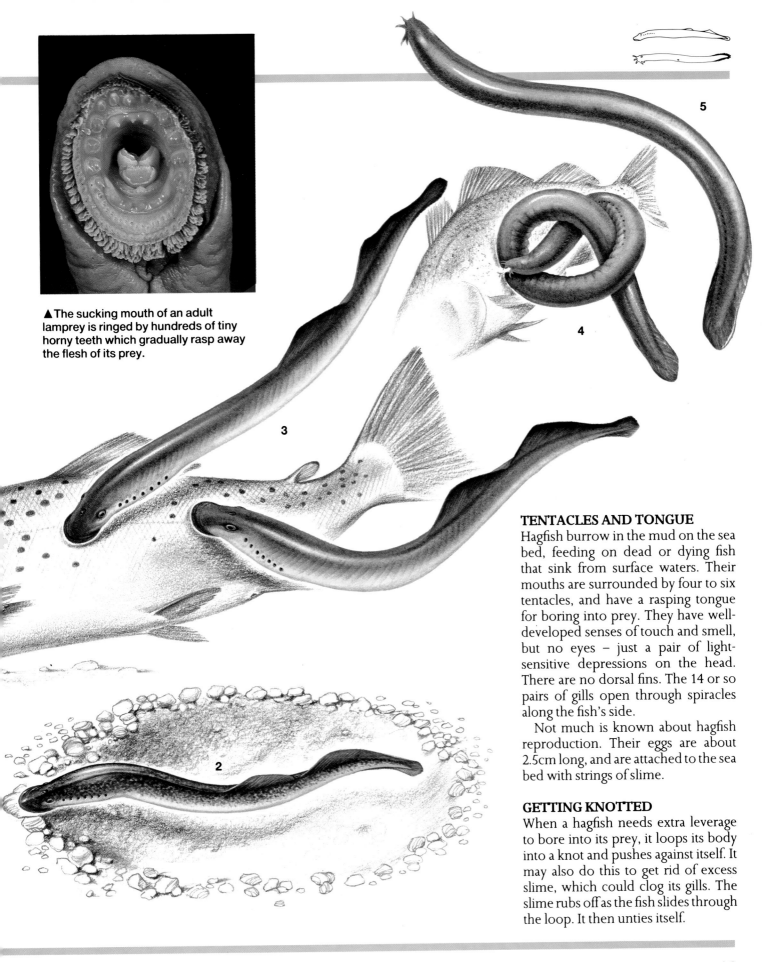

▲The sucking mouth of an adult lamprey is ringed by hundreds of tiny horny teeth which gradually rasp away the flesh of its prey.

TENTACLES AND TONGUE

Hagfish burrow in the mud on the sea bed, feeding on dead or dying fish that sink from surface waters. Their mouths are surrounded by four to six tentacles, and have a rasping tongue for boring into prey. They have well-developed senses of touch and smell, but no eyes – just a pair of light-sensitive depressions on the head. There are no dorsal fins. The 14 or so pairs of gills open through spiracles along the fish's side.

Not much is known about hagfish reproduction. Their eggs are about 2.5cm long, and are attached to the sea bed with strings of slime.

GETTING KNOTTED

When a hagfish needs extra leverage to bore into its prey, it loops its body into a knot and pushes against itself. It may also do this to get rid of excess slime, which could clog its gills. The slime rubs off as the fish slides through the loop. It then unties itself.

SHARKS, RAYS, SKATES

A coral reef glows in the shafts of sunlight filtering through the deep blue water. Red and orange corals sway in the current, and small shoals of brightly coloured fish dart in and out among them in search of food. Suddenly, a shadow falls on the reef as a Reef shark glides past, its fins scarcely moving, the water undisturbed by it passage. It sees a diver and swerves, revealing its pale underparts and the curve of its huge mouth.

Scientists group sharks and their close relatives, the rays, skates and chimaeras, separately from other fish. This is because their skeletons are made of cartilage instead of bone. Their slit-like gill openings and rough bumpy scales distinguish them from all other classes of fish. Sharks (Subclass Selachii), which are dealt with first here, include some of the largest fish in the world. The biggest of all, the Whale shark, reaches a record length of 12.65m and weighs up to 15 tonnes.

HUNTERS AND GENTLE GIANTS

Sharks are found in oceans all over the world, but are most common in the tropics and sub-tropics. Only the sleeper sharks live permanently in cold Arctic waters, where they feed on other fish and seals. Many species migrate from the tropics to temperate waters in summer. A few even invade rivers: the Bull shark has been found up to 1,600km inland in the Zambesi and Mississippi rivers.

Most sharks have more or less torpedo-shaped, streamlined bodies, with two prominent dorsal fins on their backs, and a forked tail. When swimming near the surface, the largest dorsal fin often breaks the surface, warning human swimmers of the danger below. The most streamlined sharks are fast swimmers and fierce predators, feeding mainly on other fish and squid. Several of the largest sharks, such as the Basking and Whale sharks, are harmless and feed mainly on tiny animals and plants called plankton. The Basking shark grows to 9m long and can weigh 5 tonnes.

ON THE SEABED

Some sharks spend most of their time on the seabed, feeding on shellfish (crustaceans and molluscs). They have flattened bodies and are quite sluggish swimmers. The cat, nurse, and carpet sharks use their pectoral fins to "walk" on the ocean floor. The angel sharks and the wobbegong of Australia are so flattened that they look more like rays than sharks. They usually have a camouflage colouring in the form of mottled browns and greys to conceal them as they lie in wait for their prey.

MYSTERIOUS SHAPES

A few species of shark have strange shapes the purpose of which is still unknown. Each sawshark has a long narrow snout with a row of saw-like

---

SHARKS, RAYS, SKATES Class Chondrichthyes (about 440 species)

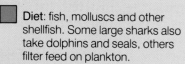 **Habitat:** mainly sea water but some in fresh water.

Diet: fish, molluscs and other shellfish. Some large sharks also take dolphins and seals, others filter feed on plankton.

Distribution: worldwide.

Breeding: internal fertilization; 2-80 eggs. Some lay eggs in horny cases, others retain eggs inside the female until after hatching; in live-bearers, up to 40 young may be born at a time.

Size: length 60cm-12.65m.

Colour: shades of brown, grey and blue, often with camouflage markings.

Species mentioned in text:
Basking shark (*Cetorhinus maximus*)
Blue shark (*Prionace glauca*)
Blue-spotted stingray (*Taeniura lymma*)
Bull shark (*Carcharhinus leucas*)
Common skate (*Raja batis*)
Dogfish (*Scyliorhinus scyliorhinus*)
Great white shark (*Carcharodon carcharias*)
Grey sharks (*Carcharhinus* species)
Hammerhead sharks (*Sphyrna* species)
Little skate (*Raja erinacea*)
Luminous shark (*Isistius brasiliensis*)
Mako shark (*Isurus oxyrhinchus*)
Pacific manta ray (*Manta hamiltoni*)
Porbeagle shark (*Lamna nasus*)
Reef shark (*Carcharhinus menisorrah*)
Sand tiger sharks (*Odontaspis* species)
Sawfish (*Pristis pristis*)
Sleeper sharks (*Somniosus* species)
Soupfin shark (*Galeorhinus zyopterus*)
Tiger shark (*Galeocerdo cuvier*)
Torpedo rays (*Torpedo* species)
Whale shark (*Rhincodon typus*)
Wobbegong (*Orectolobus maculatus*)

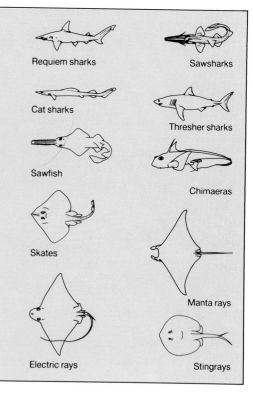

Requiem sharks

Sawsharks

Cat sharks

Thresher sharks

Sawfish

Chimaeras

Skates

Manta rays

Electric rays

Stingrays

teeth along each side. Since the shark feeds on shellfish, the saw cannot be much use for hunting, and is probably used in defence. Even stranger are the huge hammerhead sharks. Scientists now think their large heads contain organs for detecting faint pulses of electricity coming from their prey.

ROWS AND ROWS OF TEETH

In most parts of the world, sharks are feared for their savage bites. Although made of cartilage, their jaws are very strong – the Great white shark can bite through a man's arm or leg in one go. Its bite is 300 times more powerful than a human's.

In most sharks, all of the teeth are triangular in shape, and razor-sharp. A shark has many rows of teeth in its mouth. It can grow new teeth every few days if necessary. As those in front wear down, others move forward from the row behind to take their place, so that the shark always has a set of good sharp teeth. At any one time, a shark may have up to 3,000 teeth in its mouth, arranged in 6 to 20 rows. It may use over 20,000 during its lifetime. Usually only the first two rows are used for feeding. As the shark grows larger, its teeth get bigger too. A Great white shark 6.4m long may have teeth 5cm long.

▲The Great white shark is a formidable predator, attacking dolphins, porpoises and seals as well as other fish and, rarely, people.

Some sharks have teeth specialized for a particular diet. Fish-eaters have very long thin teeth to grip their slippery prey. Species that feed mainly on hard-shelled crustaceans and molluscs often have flat teeth for grinding and crushing shells.

GARBAGE COLLECTORS

Sharks will eat almost anything. An astonishing collection of items has been found in the stomachs of some

Tiger sharks – old boots, cans of paint, car licence plates, dead dogs, and human arms and legs. In 1799, an American rebel ship was chased by a British man-o'-war. The Yankee captain threw overboard his ship's papers in order to avoid being identified. The papers were later recovered from the stomach of a recently caught shark, and the captain was sent to prison.

MAN-EATERS

There are many accounts of sharks attacking people, often fatally injuring them. However, the chances of being attacked by a shark are far less than the chance of being struck by lightning. Each year humans kill tens of thousands of sharks, yet fewer than 100 humans are attacked by these fish.

Only about 10 per cent of shark species attack humans. These include the Mako, Tiger and hammerhead sharks. The most feared is the Great white shark. This reaches a length of 12m and a weight of 1,135kg. Attacks are most common in warm waters, especially off the Australian coast.

Sharks are not particularly attracted to humans – their smell is unfamiliar. Most probably the shark mistakes the flailing legs and arms of swimmer for the flippers of a seal or the fins of a large fish. Sharks are attracted to blood, however, and an injured swimmer is in serious danger. So is an angler who trails fish bait behind his or her boat in shallow water, and a spear fisherman who carries his wounded catch with him in a net.

FINDING FOOD

Many sharks have poor eyesight, but they have an excellent sense of smell. A shark can detect one part of blood in a million parts of water – equivalent to 1 drop diluted in 115 litres. They are also very sensitive to vibrations in the water, which might be caused by the movements of potential prey.

Sharks usually kill their prey by taking large jagged bites out of them,

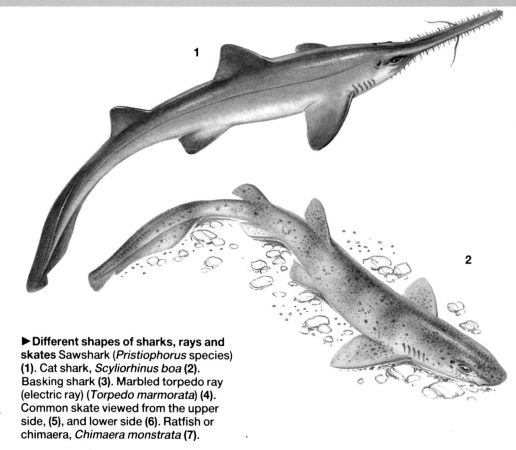

▶ **Different shapes of sharks, rays and skates** Sawshark (*Pristiophorus* species) **(1)**. Cat shark, *Scyliorhinus boa* **(2)**. Basking shark **(3)**. Marbled torpedo ray (electric ray) (*Torpedo marmorata*) **(4)**. Common skate viewed from the upper side, **(5)**, and lower side **(6)**. Ratfish or chimaera, *Chimaera monstrata* **(7)**.

then waiting while the victim bleeds to death. Thresher sharks, however, first stun their prey with blows from their very long powerful tails. Several threshers work together to drive fish into shallow water, lashing their tails to concentrate the fish into a group.

SILENT SWIMMERS

Sharks are skilful swimmers. They are propelled by their powerful tails, and glide through the water with no telltale ripples or bubbles to give away their approach. They use their large pectoral fins for tilting down or up, twisting and turning, and braking. Sharks have no air-filled swimbladders, so they must keep swimming to avoid sinking. But they do have oily livers. Oil is lighter than water, and helps to make the fish buoyant. The Basking shark used to be hunted for its oil, which was used in lamps. The liver of a medium-sized Basking shark can yield up to 900 litres of oil.

▲ A dogfish in its egg capsule, ready to emerge. The female dogfish lays 18 to 29 eggs, each measuring about 5cm wide and 11cm long. The curly tendrils anchor the egg-case to rocks or seaweeds. The young fish hatches after about 9 months.

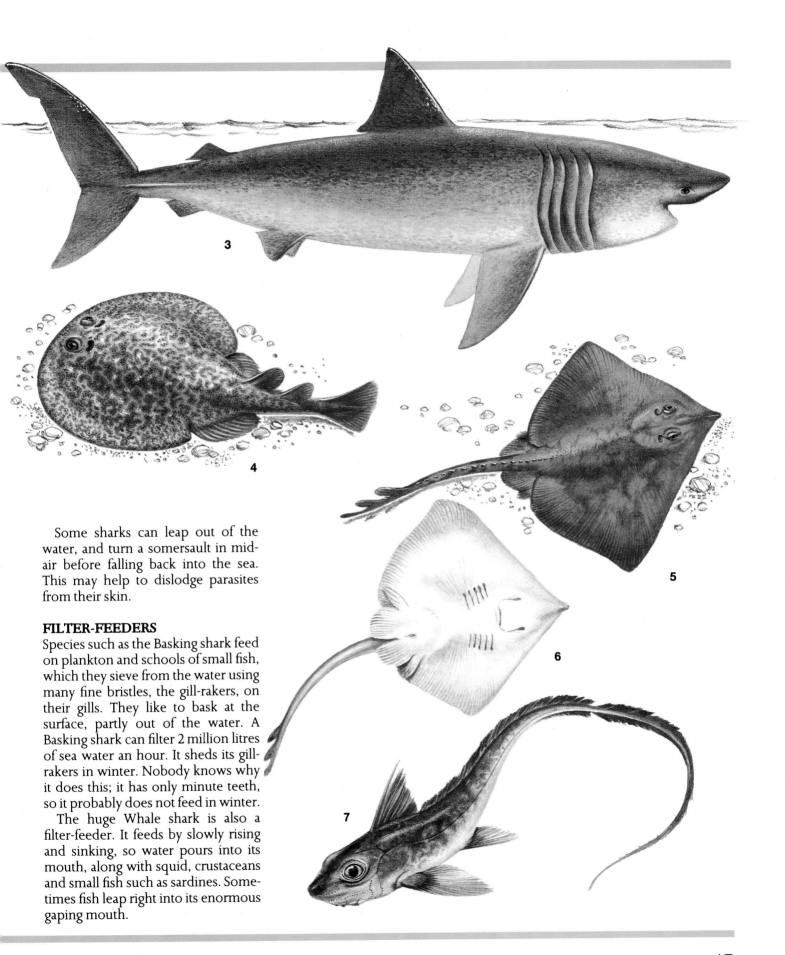

Some sharks can leap out of the water, and turn a somersault in mid-air before falling back into the sea. This may help to dislodge parasites from their skin.

FILTER-FEEDERS

Species such as the Basking shark feed on plankton and schools of small fish, which they sieve from the water using many fine bristles, the gill-rakers, on their gills. They like to bask at the surface, partly out of the water. A Basking shark can filter 2 million litres of sea water an hour. It sheds its gill-rakers in winter. Nobody knows why it does this; it has only minute teeth, so it probably does not feed in winter.

The huge Whale shark is also a filter-feeder. It feeds by slowly rising and sinking, so water pours into its mouth, along with squid, crustaceans and small fish such as sardines. Sometimes fish leap right into its enormous gaping mouth.

DIAMOND-SHAPED DESIGNS

Rays and skates (Order Batiformes, about 320 species) are very flattened fish that live on the sand and mud at the bottom of seas and rivers. There they prey on molluscs, crustaceans and other fish. They also feed on dead animal remains, and help to keep the seabed clean. Most species lie in wait for their quarry, but the manta rays feed by sifting plankton and small fish from the water. Electric rays stun fish with electric shocks, while eagle rays get at shellfish by squirting water from their mouths to blast away the sand. They can excavate holes 30cm deep.

Rays and skates have no anal fin. The pectoral fins are fused to the sides of the head well in front of the gill slits. Many species have both a longish snout – giving them a diamond shape – and a long narrow tail. In some, the tail is armed with poisonous spines for defence. The mouth and gill slits are on the underside of the body. Water enters the gills through a large opening, the spiracle, on the top of the head behind the eyes. When resting, skates may raise their heads just above the seabed and take in water through the mouth too.

FLYING UNDERWATER

Rays and skates are found in most parts of the oceans. A few species live as deep as 6,000m, while some South American species live in rivers. They range in size from the Little skate, which grows to 50cm long, to the 7m-wide, 1,360kg Pacific manta ray.

The huge pectoral fins of rays and skates are often referred to as wings. When swimming, manta rays and eagle rays flap these up and down. Skates and stingrays "fly" through the water using a wave-like movement of their pectoral fins from front to rear.

▶The underside of a Common skate showing the large mouth, the nostrils (looking rather like eyes), the gill slits, and the rather muscular pelvic fins.

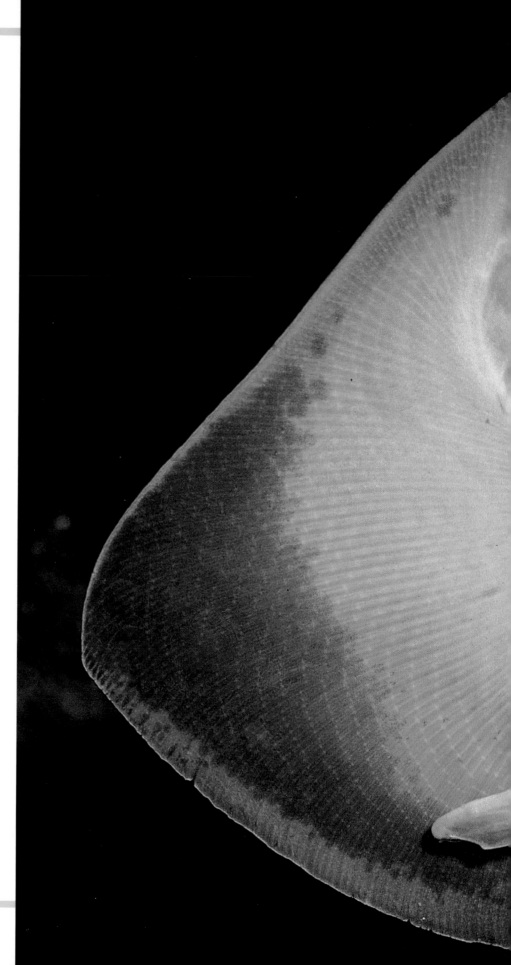

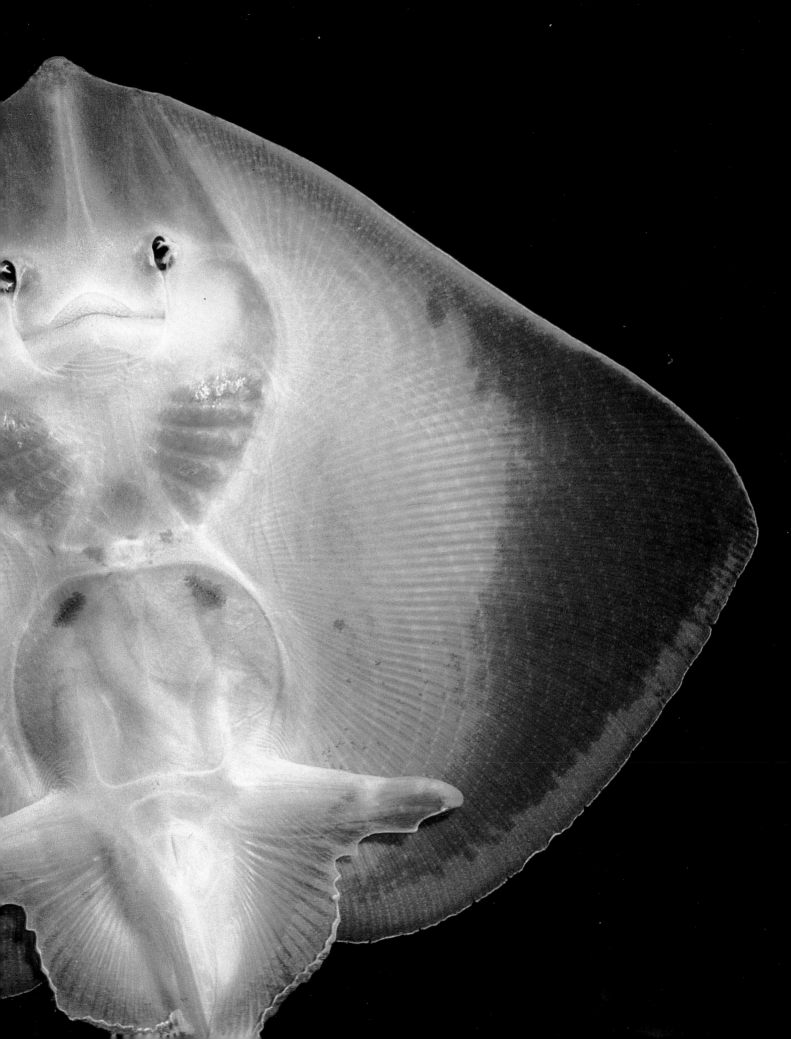

OCEAN DEVIL

The Pacific manta ray may have a "wingspan" over 6m. Two fins project from its head rather like horns, hence its common name of devil fish. It is one of the few rays to live in the open water. It feeds on crustaceans and small fish, and will often chase shoals of fish into the shallows to force them into its mouth. Manta rays make leaps out of the water, crashing back to the surface with a loud slap.

SHOCK TACTICS

Most sharks and rays have organs on their heads, near their eyes, which can detect faint pulses of electricity. As a

▲ Spread like a butterfly, this eagle ray, *Aetobatus narinari*, inhabits tropical and sub-tropical waters.

fish moves in water, it sets up a weak electric field, which the shark can detect. These are the most sensitive electric organs known in nature. Electric rays and torpedo rays can also produce electricity, and use it to stun their prey. They can give quite powerful shocks of up to 60 volts.

SAWS, SPINES AND BEAKS

The sawfish, up to 6m long, looks more like a shark than a ray, with large dorsal fins and small pectoral fins. Its

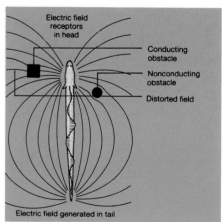

▲ An electric fish produces an electric field around itself, which is disturbed by objects in the water.

◀The sawfish's snout is a multi-purpose tool, used for digging, killing and defence. The large spiracles behind the eyes are used to let water into the gill chambers.

▼A Blue-spotted stingray swims over the seabed. The spines on its tail are armed with poison.

amazing snout is armed with 12 to 30 pairs of saw-like teeth, and has many uses. It can slash at shoals of fish, stunning or killing them. It can impale several fish at a time, which are later scraped off on the seabed and eaten. The saw is also used to dig in the mud for shellfish. It is a valuable defence, too, and can inflict lethal wounds on enemies many times larger than the sawfish, such as some whales.

The ratfish (Subclass Holocephali, about 23 species), often called rabbit-fish or chimaeras, are relatives of sharks that live in cold water down to depths of 2,400m. They feed on the seabed, propping themselves up on the tips of their fins. They have blunt heads with large metallic blue-green eyes, and very prominent lateral line systems on the head and sides. The large dorsal fin is tipped with poison-ous spines. Their teeth are fused together to form a bird-like beak which the fish use to crush the shells of molluscs and crustaceans. Male ratfish have an extra pair of claspers on their heads, which may be used to grip the female during mating.

BABY IN A BAG

Sharks and rays have some very un-usual methods of reproduction. They all perform internal fertilization; the male's pelvic fins possess a pair of claspers on their inner edges, which form a tube down which sperm is passed into the female during mating. They produce relatively few eggs, but the young are well-developed when they hatch or are born.

Skates and some sharks lay each of their eggs in a horny case, called a sea purse or mermaid's purse. Safe inside, the embryo feeds on the yolk and reaches a good size before hatching. The empty purses can often be found washed up on the seashore.

In many sharks, stingrays and the sawfish the eggs remain safe inside the female until they hatch. In some species the newly hatched fish then feed on the yolks of any remaining unfertilized eggs before escaping to the water outside. In the sand tiger sharks, from six to eight embryos are formed, which then eat one another until only two are left.

In a few sharks, such as the grey, Blue and hammerhead species, a kind of placenta (fleshy growth containing blood vessels) develops to link the young shark embryo to the mother's blood vessels to bring food to it, rather like mammal embryos are fed. This ensures that the young sharks are well-developed and able to hunt well soon after they are born.

LUMINOUS SHARKS

The Luminous shark, which lives in tropical and sub-tropical waters, gives off a bright green light from the underside of its body. Some spiny dogfish that live in deep water also have light-producing organs along the sides of their bodies. The light may serve to attract prey – mostly squid – or it may be a kind of camouflage, hiding the dogfish's dark silhouette from predators lurking below.

FOR FOOD AND SPORT

Only a few sharks, for example the spiny dogfish and the Soupfin shark, are fished in large numbers for food. But some, such as the thresher, Mako and Porbeagle sharks, are popular sport fish because they put up such a good fight when hooked. Other sharks and rays are a nuisance to fishermen, taking bites out of fish caught in nets or on hooks.

STURGEONS, PADDLEFISH

A sturgeon swims slowly over the river bed, its large shadow blackening the mud. It moves stiffly, as if its bony armour is weighing it down. Little eddies of mud swirl up into the water as the sturgeon's long feelers probe the bottom, its large rubbery mouth eager to scoop up any small water creatures it dislodges. Now that spring is warming the water, it needs to feed well, ready for its journey up-river to spawn.

Sturgeons and paddlefish are living fossils, the only survivors of an ancient group of bony fish. (Fossils of their ancestors have been found in rocks 135 million years old.) They have very long, spindle-shaped bodies with long snouts. The mouth is on the underside, as these fish feed on the bottom of rivers, lakes and seas. The very young fish may have small soft teeth, but the adults have no teeth. There are no proper scales, except along the top edge of the tail fin, but sturgeons have five rows of large bony plates running along the body.

BIG-NOSED FISH

Paddlefish live in large muddy rivers, for example the Mississippi in North America and the Yangtse and Hwang-ho in China. The exact function of their long paddle-shaped snout is unknown. It may be used to balance the huge gaping mouth, as a shovel for digging in the mud, a scoop, or even as a beater to knock small animals off underwater plants. Alternatively, it may function as a sense organ, detecting the movements of small water animals by the tiny electrical fields they generate. This use of electricity is found in other kinds of fish that live in muddy water.

A paddlefish feeds by swimming along near the water surface with its huge mouth open, scooping up tiny floating shellfish and various other invertebrates. It feeds mainly at night, and rests at the bottom of deep pools during the day. To spawn, paddlefish move upstream to shallower water. Their eggs are eaten as caviar, though they are not so highly prized as those of their relatives, the sturgeons.

STURGEONS, PADDLEFISH Order
Acipenseriformes (*27 species*)

Habitat: sturgeons: rivers, lakes and oceans; paddlefish: large muddy rivers.

Diet: small invertebrates.

Distribution: sturgeons: Caspian Sea and North Atlantic, North Pacific and Arctic oceans and associated rivers; paddlefish: Mississippi, Yangtse and Hwang-ho rivers and their tributaries.

Breeding: lay large numbers of eggs on the river bed. Migrate to special spawning areas.

Size: length 75cm-9m.

Colour: brownish- or greenish-grey.

Species mentioned in text:
Beluga or Russian sturgeon (*Huso huso*)
Chinese paddlefish (*Psephurus gladius*)
Paddlefish (*Polyodon spathula*)
Sterlet (*Acipenser ruthenus*)

Sturgeons   Paddlefish

▼The sterlet, a species of sturgeon, has become a popular, but rather expensive, aquarium fish. It is difficult to feed as its favourite food is finely ground mussels.

LONG-LIVED GIANTS

Sturgeons are among the largest freshwater fish in the world, and are said to live for over 150 years. The largest sturgeon known, a Beluga or Russian sturgeon, was over 80 years old, 8.5m long and weighed more than 1,300kg. Some species of sturgeon live in the sea, but breed in fresh water. Others live entirely in fresh water – in rivers, lakes and inland seas.

These fish feed on animals that live in the beds of rivers and seas – small fish, worms, shellfish, molluscs and other invertebrates. They use their long shovel-shaped snout to push into the bottom sediments. On the underside of the snout are four thin fleshy tentacles called barbels, which the sturgeons use to feel for food in the muddy water. The mouth lies just behind the barbels.

LIVING CAVIAR

Sturgeons used to be much prized for their very tasty flesh. They were once common in both North American and European waters, but have declined mainly due to over-hunting and water pollution. Today, sturgeon hunting is banned in most countries.

Even more desirable than their flesh are their eggs, the famous caviar. In the breeding season, all sturgeons migrate to favourite spawning areas. River sturgeons move downstream, while sea sturgeons migrate to continental rivers or to protected coasts. They stop feeding while they spawn. A female sturgeon may produce over 3 million eggs, which stick to underwater plants. Commercially, the fish are caught and stripped of eggs. A Beluga sturgeon caught in 1926 weighed 1,000kg and yielded 180kg of caviar.

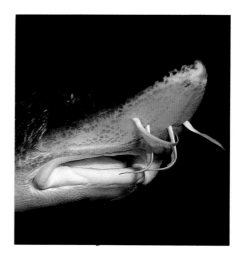

▲ The sturgeon uses its shovel-shaped snout and flexible tentacles (barbels) to probe for food in mud.

▼ The paddlefish is a filter-feeder. It sieves food from the water with special combs on its gills.

COELACANTH, LUNGFISH

In the depths of the Indian Ocean, around the Comoro Islands, is a dimly lit world of black knobbly rocks and pale coral sand. Here, a huge dark fish drifts slowly over the ocean floor, its strange lobed fins rotating slowly like propellers. The coelacanth is searching for its prey.

The coelacanth and lungfish are not related to one another, but they are all descendants of fish whose fossils have been found in rocks over 400 million years old, and they look very much like them. Some of their ancestors gave rise to the first four-footed land animals, the amphibians.

DISCOVERY OF THE CENTURY
Fossil coelacanths represent fish that lived in the oceans throughout the Age of the Dinosaurs, but until 1938 scientists assumed that they, too, had died out about 70 million years ago.

Then a group of fishermen caught a strange fish 1.5m long off the coast of South Africa. It turned out to be a

living coelacanth. Fourteen years later – after advertising among the native fishermen – it was discovered that a single species of coelacanth was still living in the deep waters between the African coast and Madagascar, near the Comoro Islands. Many specimens have now been sent to museums, and the fish has even been filmed in its natural habitat using a submarine.

A LIVING FOSSIL
So what makes the coelacanth so special? Just a cursory examination shows how it differs from modern fish. It is a large fish, up to 1.8m long. Its paired fins have stiff fleshy bases rather like stubby limbs. In fact, the coelacanth is sometimes called a lobe-finned fish. Each lobe has its own skeleton and muscles, and is rather strong. The tail is wide and thick, with a middle lobe that can wiggle independently so that the tail appears to have three parts. The fish's deep blue body is covered in large, heavy scales, which local people use as scrapers.

Not much is known about coelacanth reproduction. The females are larger than the males. Each produces 20 large eggs, about the size of tennis balls. Females have been found containing young, so they must give birth to live young. Scientists think the female carries the young for about a year before giving birth.

◀The coelacanth has a large mouth armed with spiky teeth, and feeds on other fish. Why it inhabits the sea when fossil coelacanths lived in fresh water; why it is found only around the Comoro Islands; and why only one species has survived – all remain a mystery.

COELACANTH, LUNGFISH Coelacanth: Order Coelacanthiformes (*1 species*); Lungfish: Order Dipteriformes (*6 species*).

▪️

〰️ **Habitat:** coelacanth: oceans; lungfish: fresh water.

▪️ **Diet:** fish and invertebrates.

Distribution: coelacanth: Indian Ocean around Comoro Islands; lungfish: South America, Africa and Australia.

Breeding: coelacanth: about 20 eggs, live birth; lungfish: up to 5,000 eggs; lays on mud or in nest in mud.

Size: length up to 2m.

Colour: coelacanth: dark blue with white blotches; lungfish: brown or dark grey, with paler underside.

Species mentioned in text:
African lungfish (*Protopterus* species)
Australian lungfish (*Neoceratodus forsteri*)
Coelacanth (*Latimeria chalumnae*)
South American lungfish (*Lepidosiren paradoxa*)

Coelacanth

Lungfish

FISH THAT BREATHE AIR

The ancestors of lungfish lived in swamps 350 million years ago. Today, lungfish inhabit rivers and lakes in warm parts of the world. They feed on other fish, using a pair of sharp scissor-like plates instead of teeth. They have gills just like other fish, but they also possess "lungs" for breathing air. These are special pouches leading off the gut.

The Australian lungfish is the most primitive species. It has large scales and its fins are lobed like those of the coelacanth. It grows up to 1.5m long, and has well-developed gills, but only one lung. It cannot survive drought and uses its lung only when the water becomes stale or dirty.

The African and South American lungfish have more eel-like bodies, and their fins resemble long fleshy feelers. They have smaller scales, and two lungs. When their watery home dries out, they burrow in the soft mud and sleep until rain falls again, using their lungs to breathe air that diffuses through the mud. The African lungfish all secrete a cocoon of mucus around themselves, which hardens and prevents their bodies drying out.

Male African and South American lungfish build a nest 50 to 80cm deep in the mud, and persuade several females to lay eggs in it. The male stays with the eggs to guard them. Young lungfish have external gills when they hatch. These are absorbed as the lungs and internal gills develop.

▲The lines of tiny holes on this South American lungfish's head are part of the fish's lateral line system, which detects vibrations in the water.

▼▶An African lungfish sleeps in its mucus cocoon. Air reaches it through a hole at the top. Here, the lungfish can survive for up to 4 years, feeding off its own muscle tissue. When the pool fills with water again, the cocoon dissolves and the fish emerges.

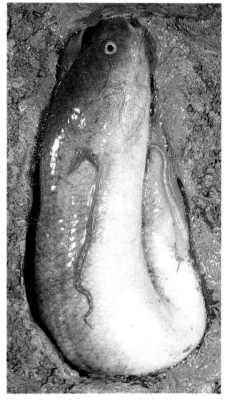

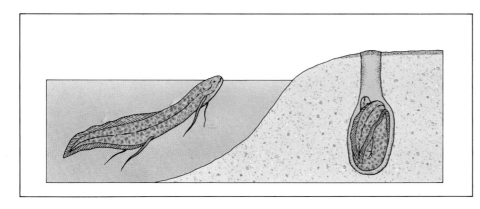

BOWFIN, GARFISH

In the shallow Sun-dappled waters of a North American lake, a Longnose gar waits motionless beside a rotting log. It is so well camouflaged that it looks like a piece of wood. A metre or so away, a trout swims into view. The gar starts to edge forward, the movements of its fins so slight that its disguise remains convincing. Suddenly it seizes the trout with an alligator-like swipe of its long jaws.

The bowfin and the garfish species all live in shallow weed-filled freshwater. Here the oxygen supply in the water becomes scarce in warm weather. The fish come to the surface to gulp air, which goes into their swimbladder. This provides buoyancy and acts as a lung. They also have large, thick armour-like scales.

ALLIGATOR SNOUTS

Garfish have jaws armed with many needle-sharp teeth for seizing their slippery prey, which range from fish and frogs to waterbirds. In winter, garfish rest in deeper water. In spring, they move to the shallow water to spawn. The eggs stick to sand, mud and water weeds.

Young garfish do not resemble their parents. They use a sticky disc at the front of the mouth to cling to plants while they feed on their yolk sacs. They grow fast, and within 2 weeks are good free-swimming predators.

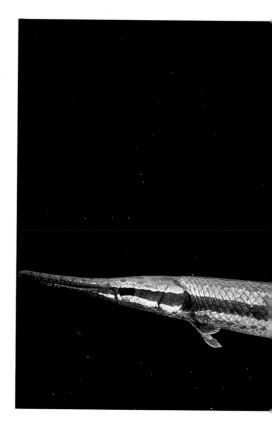

BOWFIN, GARFISH

Bowfin: Order Amiiformes (*1 species*);
Garfish: Order Lepisosteiformes
(*7 species*)

 Habitat: rivers and lakes.

 Diet: fish, frogs and invertebrates.

Distribution: North America from Great Lakes south to Central America, Cuba.

Breeding: in spring, in shallow water. Male bowfin makes nest in mud lined with roots; garfish do not make nests. Up to 30,000 adhesive eggs. Male bowfin guards eggs and young.

Size: bowfin: length 45-100cm, females larger than males; garfish: length 75cm-4m (Alligator gar).

Colour: olive-green, brown or grey, with darker blotches. Some garfish have a dark stripe along the sides. Bowfin males, and sometimes females, have large dark spot on tail.

Species mentioned in text:
Alligator gar (*Atractosteus spatula*)
Bowfin (*Amia calva*)
Longnose gar (*Lepisosteus osseus*)

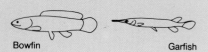

Bowfin   Garfish

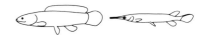

▲ The bowfin swims slowly as it hunts. It can accelerate rapidly to seize its prey.

◄ The Longnose gar has a dark stripe along each side of its body which conceals its eyes and improves its camouflage.

▼ This garfish looks smooth and sleek because its scales do not overlap, but fit together like bricks in a wall.

LAZY BUT EFFICIENT KILLER

The bowfin is a fierce predator. It feeds on fish, frogs, shrimps and water insects. Although it is not good to eat, some fishermen enjoy the battle involved in catching a bowfin. Like the garfish, it relies on stealth to catch its prey. Its common name comes from the long wavy dorsal fin which runs along much of its back.

The bowfin's body is covered in overlapping scales. The males have a large black spot ringed with bright orange near the top of the tail base. The lung allows the bowfin to live in foul water where no other predators can survive. The fish can survive for up to a day out of water.

CARING FATHERS

In spring, the male bowfin becomes more brightly coloured, and his belly turns orange. He moves to shallow water and makes a saucer-shaped nest 30 to 60cm across in the mud. Each male fiercely defends his nest against other males, but he allows several females to lay their eggs in it. The male guards the eggs and fans them to keep them aerated.

After 8 to 10 days the eggs hatch, and the transparent young fish larvae cling to the water weeds, using a sticky pad on their snouts. Once they have used up their yolk sacs, they stay together in a shoal, still guarded by their father.

EELS, TARPONS

In the warm, shallow waters off the Red Sea coast, patches of sunlight dancing across the pale coral sand illuminate a strange garden. Speckled tendrils sway in the current, bending towards the oncoming water. But these are not plants. As the shadow of a large fish falls over the sand, the garden eels vanish into their burrows. When the Sun once more touches their burrows, the eels emerge.

Eels are the most snake-like of all fish, with long cylindrical bodies and long, narrow fins that seem scarcely to interrupt their body outline. These fins do not have stiff supporting rays, but are soft and flexible. While most fish have about 30 spinal bones, some freshwater eels have as many as 260.

Eels are ideally shaped for sliding in and out of crevices, or burrowing into soft sand or mud. This is their main defence. Also, eels all appear to be almost naked – the scales of most species are tiny – and a thick slime covers the skin, making them hard to grasp and often distasteful to eat.

WIDESPREAD AND VARIED

Eels are found all over the world in oceans and seas, from the coast to the cold dark depths several kilometres beneath the surface. A few species also live in fresh water, but these return to the sea to breed.

Most eels are predators, preying on other fish, crustaceans, molluscs and worms. A few are parasitic as adults, feeding on other fish – mainly the sick or dying. The teeth of eels vary according to their diet. Those that feed on very small water animals have teeth like fine brushes, while larger predators have vicious fangs. Eels that specialize in eating shellfish have flat teeth for crushing and chewing.

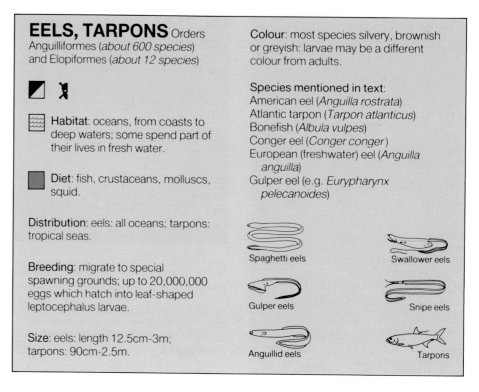

EELS, TARPONS Orders
Anguilliformes (*about 600 species*)
and Elopiformes (*about 12 species*)

Habitat: oceans, from coasts to deep waters; some spend part of their lives in fresh water.

Diet: fish, crustaceans, molluscs, squid.

Distribution: eels: all oceans; tarpons: tropical seas.

Breeding: migrate to special spawning grounds; up to 20,000,000 eggs which hatch into leaf-shaped leptocephalus larvae.

Size: eels: length 12.5cm-3m; tarpons: 90cm-2.5m.

Colour: most species silvery, brownish or greyish: larvae may be a different colour from adults.

Species mentioned in text:
American eel (*Anguilla rostrata*)
Atlantic tarpon (*Tarpon atlanticus*)
Bonefish (*Albula vulpes*)
Conger eel (*Conger conger*)
European (freshwater) eel (*Anguilla anguilla*)
Gulper eel (e.g. *Eurypharynx pelecanoides*)

Spaghetti eels
Swallower eels
Gulper eels
Snipe eels
Anguillid eels
Tarpons

BLOODHOUNDS OF THE SEA

Eels have the best sense of smell of all fish. Large nasal chambers lined with smell detectors stretch from the nostrils at the tip of the snout almost to the eyes. The European freshwater eel can detect 1 part of chemical in 1 million million million parts of water, the equivalent of detecting a molecule of scent in each nasal chamber.

MENACING MORAYS

Moray eels include some of the largest – up to 3m long – and most dangerous eels. Like the equally large Conger eel, they live on rocky coasts and on coral reefs in tropical and sub-tropical regions. By day they hide in crevices and underwater caves, where they lie partly concealed, watching the ocean world go by. Moray eels have thick leathery skin, and often have brilliant colours and markings. When open, their huge mouths extend back behind their eyes. They have a pair of conspicuous tubular nostrils near the front of the snout, and another smaller pair near the eyes.

▶ Moray eels spend most of the day guarding the entrance to their favourite crevices and looking out for passing prey. Their thick skin extends over the fins, making them difficult to distinguish.

Moray eels are very bad-tempered fish, and can inflict nasty bites on divers that approach too close. The wounds are deep, and easily become infected. Despite their evil reputation, moray eels do not feed on large prey. Their attacks on divers are usually the result of surprise or provocation. They hunt at night for fish and all types of shellfish.

In the ancient Roman world, moray eels were a sign of wealth. They were kept in captivity, and displayed by the hundred at banquets. The family of the moray eels, Muraenidae, is named after a wealthy Roman, Licinius Muraena, who lived in the second century BC and was famous for his captive morays. These eels are good to eat, and are caught for food in the Far East and the Mediterranean region.

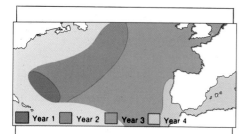

Year 1 | Year 2 | Year 3 | Year 4

▲European eels hatch from eggs laid in the Sargasso Sea, then drift as leptocephali on the Gulf Stream until they reach the coasts and rivers of Europe.

▼Most eels have transparent leaf-like larvae called leptocephali. In some species these grow very large: those of the deep-sea spiny eels grow up to 183cm long before shrinking and changing into adults.

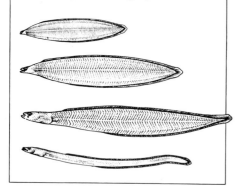

▼A European freshwater eel, stranded by receding flood waters, wriggles overland in search of water.

GIANT EARTHWORMS?

Freshwater eels are found along the coasts and in the rivers and lakes of most continents, except for the west coasts of America and along the south Atlantic coasts. They hide by day and come out to feed at night.

Until the last century, no juvenile freshwater eels had ever been found, and there were many theories as to how the fish reproduced. The ancient Greek philosopher Aristotle thought that the eels were born from earthworms that were created in the mud. Later, scientists believed they were born from a small fish, which in German is still called Aalmutter – the eel-mother. Then in 1777 an Italian, Mondini, found eel eggs.

TRANSPARENT YOUNG

By the early 1800s everyone believed that freshwater eels mate and spawn (lay eggs), but they had not found where the fish met to do this. Then, strange transparent leaf-like fish called leptocephali (meaning thin heads) were caught off the coasts of Europe. When these fish were kept in an aquarium, they slowly changed into eels. The leptocephali were the larvae of freshwater eels.

MYSTERIES OF MIGRATION

Early this century, the Danish scientist Johannes Schmidt tracked leptocephali back across the Atlantic Ocean, looking for smaller and yet smaller (younger) larvae. On reaching the Sargasso Sea, just to the north of the Caribbean islands, he found newly hatched larvae. Thus the spawning grounds of the European freshwater eel were discovered and its amazing life story was revealed.

In spring, the adult eels spawn at depths of about 400m in the Sargasso Sea and then they die. The tiny larvae, called glass fish, drift eastwards almost 5,000km on the Gulf Stream currents until they reach the rivers of Europe. The journey takes them up to 3 years.

How they navigate is a mystery, but they may be well be able to follow the Earth's magnetic field.

Nobody knows exactly how the leptocephali feed and grow on this journey. They have strange forward-pointing teeth on the outside of their jaws, and no food has ever been found in their stomachs. Perhaps they absorb through their skin vital nutrients and minerals from the sea water.

The life cycle of the American eel is similar. It breeds in the western part of the Sargasso and its leptocephali take only 1 or 2 years to reach fresh waters.

Why the eels should have evolved such a long migration is a mystery. It may be that the spawning and feeding grounds became established millions of years ago, before the continents of the Americas and Europe drifted apart, and the route has lengthened as the continents have moved.

FROM GLASS TO GOLD

Once the leptocephali enter coastal waters, they change shape, develop pectoral fins and scales, and change into "elvers". The elvers migrate up-river in their thousands. On one day in 1886, 3 tonnes of elvers were caught in a single English river. These small fish can climb weirs and even struggle overland if the ground is wet enough.

Gradually the elvers develop an olive-brown colouring and yellow bellies, and become yellow eels. Their bodies are now adapted for living in fresh water, and they feed and grow in the rivers for several years. Female eels travel much further up rivers than males, which tend to stay around the river mouth. The males stop growing after about 5 years, but the females can grow for up to 15 years, and get bigger.

▶Garden eels lean into the water current to feed. Carefully spaced about 50cm apart, each eel is just out of reach of its neighbour. Garden eels seldom leave their burrows.

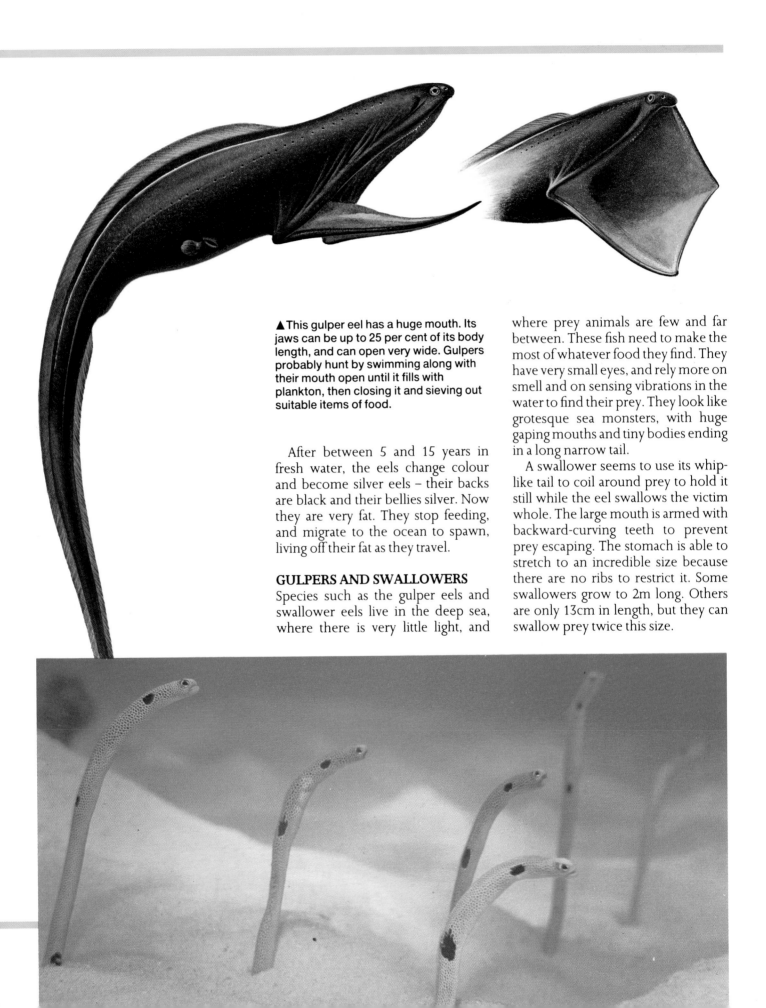

▲This gulper eel has a huge mouth. Its jaws can be up to 25 per cent of its body length, and can open very wide. Gulpers probably hunt by swimming along with their mouth open until it fills with plankton, then closing it and sieving out suitable items of food.

After between 5 and 15 years in fresh water, the eels change colour and become silver eels – their backs are black and their bellies silver. Now they are very fat. They stop feeding, and migrate to the ocean to spawn, living off their fat as they travel.

GULPERS AND SWALLOWERS

Species such as the gulper eels and swallower eels live in the deep sea, where there is very little light, and where prey animals are few and far between. These fish need to make the most of whatever food they find. They have very small eyes, and rely more on smell and on sensing vibrations in the water to find their prey. They look like grotesque sea monsters, with huge gaping mouths and tiny bodies ending in a long narrow tail.

A swallower seems to use its whip-like tail to coil around prey to hold it still while the eel swallows the victim whole. The large mouth is armed with backward-curving teeth to prevent prey escaping. The stomach is able to stretch to an incredible size because there are no ribs to restrict it. Some swallowers grow to 2m long. Others are only 13cm in length, but they can swallow prey twice this size.

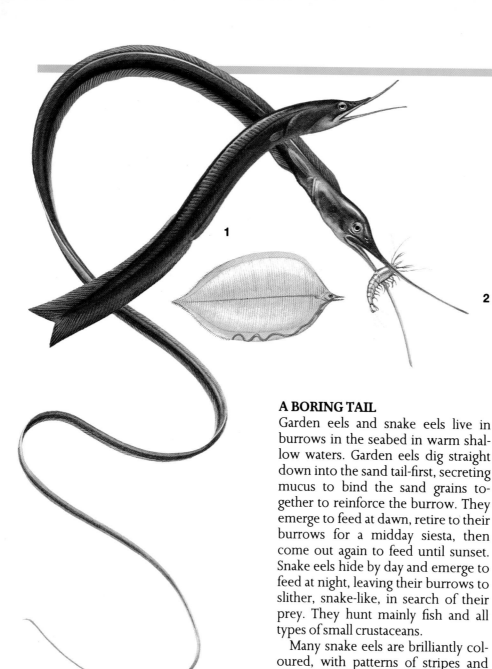

1

2

remain during the day. At maturity they leave their burrows and become shimmering, long-finned eels.

PRIMITIVE TARPONS

Tarpons and their close relative, the bonefish, are primitive fish, and look remarkably similar to the ancestors of today's bony fish.

Today, these species live in tropical seas, where they feed on other fish and squid. They have teeth on the roof of the mouth and on the tongue, as well as on the jaws. Tarpons are skilful swimmers, and rely on speed to get them out of trouble. Nicknamed "silver kings", their large silvery scales reflect light as if they are made of polished metal. The Atlantic tarpon grows up to 2.5m long and can weigh more than 130kg. The bonefish rarely grows to a weight of more than 9kg. It has a wedge-shaped snout, which it uses to dig in the mud for shellfish.

Like the eels, tarpons and the bonefish produce leptocephalus larvae. The adults migrate to the ocean to spawn, and the larvae migrate back to the coasts, where they metamorphose and grow in warm lagoons and mangrove swamps. Sadly, these nursery grounds are increasingly at risk from drainage and pollution. Their waters are often low in oxygen, but the tarpons use their swimbladders like lungs, and take oxygen from the air.

LEAPING SILVER

Tarpons are famous for making huge leaps out of the water. Since they have few predators, the reason for these leaps is not known. Tarpons are very popular with anglers as they can be caught close to the shore, and put up a fierce fight, twisting and turning and leaping into the air. They are not edible, so most catches are released.

▶A shoal of tarpons feeds around a rocky outcrop. The tarpons' gleaming scales are sometimes made into items of jewellery.

A BORING TAIL

Garden eels and snake eels live in burrows in the seabed in warm shallow waters. Garden eels dig straight down into the sand tail-first, secreting mucus to bind the sand grains together to reinforce the burrow. They emerge to feed at dawn, retire to their burrows for a midday siesta, then come out again to feed until sunset. Snake eels hide by day and emerge to feed at night, leaving their burrows to slither, snake-like, in search of their prey. They hunt mainly fish and all types of small crustaceans.

Many snake eels are brilliantly coloured, with patterns of stripes and spots. The reason for this is a mystery, since they move around only at night, when their colours cannot be appreciated. Snake eels use their stiff, sharp tails to bore into the sand or mud. This way, they can remain on guard as they burrow, ready to defend themselves with their vicious teeth.

LIVING SPAGHETTI

Some of the thinnest burrowing eels are the spaghetti, or worm, eels. These have slender, apparently scaleless and finless, bodies. They are very unusual among eels in burrowing head-first into the sand or mud, where they

▲Two species of snipe eel A Curtailed snipe eel (*Cyema atrum*), almost 15cm long, and its leptocephalus larva, 8cm long (1). A snipe eel with its prey (2). These strange deep-sea eels have long spreading jaws that cannot meet. They spend a lot of time hanging vertically in the water, mouth down. They feed on shrimps, which have long thin legs and long antennae that probably get entangled on the eels' fine teeth.

HERRINGS, ANCHOVIES

In the warm waters of the Bahamas, a shoal of sardines drifts like a cloud. The fish are so tightly packed that they seem to move as one animal. Gradually the shimmering cloud changes shape as the sardines weave in and out among the corals, unaware of the predator lurking below them. The larger fish makes its strike, and the shoal scatters.

Herrings and sardines are small silvery fish with slender streamlined bodies and deeply forked tails. They are some of the most numerous fish in the sea. They are also important food fish.

The herring family (Clupeidae) contains many familiar fish, such as shad, sardines, the pilchard, the sprat and whitebait (young herrings and sprats). It is closely related to the anchovy family (Engraulidae).

OCEAN CAMOUFLAGE

Herrings and their relatives are usually grey-green on the back and belly, and silvery along the sides. The green colour gives them good camouflage when seen from above by predators such as seagulls. Also the flashing of their mirror-like sides makes it difficult for underwater predators to pick out one fish from a moving shoal. In herrings, the belly scales form a narrow ridge such that the fish do not cast a large shadow on the water below.

FEEDING ON THE MOVE

Most herrings and anchovies feed as they swim, sieving the water though special fleshy combs (gill-rakers) on their gills to extract the tiny floating plants and animals of the plankton. Large species eat small fish. Herrings follow the movements of their prey, rising to the surface by day, and sinking with the plankton at night.

Within these two families, several species may travel huge distances, sometimes thousands of kilometres, in search of good feeding grounds. Many also breed in one area and feed in another.

SEA WOLVES AND FISH PASTE

The Wolf herring grows to a length of over 3.5m. It is a fierce predator, with large fangs for gripping its prey. It often leaps right out of the water as it tries to seize its prey, and is famous for putting up a strong fight if hooked by fishermen.

Anchovies are smaller than herrings and often only 10cm long. They have no keel of scales on their belly, and the long pointed snout hangs out over the lower jaw. Anchovies are fished in great numbers as a source of oil and meal, and they are also tinned or made into paste.

SAFETY IN NUMBERS?

Shoals of herrings and the anchovetta are often so large that they stretch for several kilometres, and may contain up to 3,000,000,000 fish. This helps to protect them from predators. When attacked, the fish swim much closer together: a shoal of anchovettas many

▼A species of herring from the Southern Hemisphere, which lives near coasts and sometimes enters rivers.

HERRINGS, ANCHOVIES Order
Clupeiformes (*about 342 species*)

■

 Habitat: sea and fresh water; some species migrate to fresh water to spawn.

 Diet: mainly plankton, small fish and soft-bodied animals.

Distribution: oceans worldwide, fresh water in Africa.

Breeding: migrate to special spawning grounds; lay up to 500,000 eggs.

Size: length up to 90 cm but most herring less than 30 cm long.

Colour: greenish, darker on back than belly, with silvery sides.

Species mentioned in text:
American shad (*Alosa sapidissima*)
Atlantic herring (*Clupea harengus*)
Anchovetta (*Engraulis ringens*)
Common anchovy (*E. encrasicolus*)
Menhaden (*Brevoortia tyrannus*)
Pilchard (*Clupea pilchardus*)
Sprat (*C. sprattus*)
Wolf herring (*Chirocentrus dorab*)

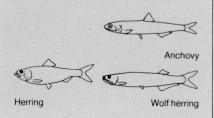

Anchovy

Herring

Wolf herring

hundred metres wide shrinks to just a few metres across. It is difficult for a predator to single out one individual to chase. Even if one is taken, this is a tiny proportion of all the fish present.

This behaviour has the opposite effect on human predators, however, as a whole shoal can be trapped in a single trawl net. Herrings are highly nutritious to eat, and are also found not too far from the shore, which makes them attractive to fishermen. In some regions, such as around North European coasts, fishing has become so efficient that stocks of herring are seriously depleted and controls have had to be introduced.

PROLIFIC BREEDERS

Herrings usually breed at a particular time of year, but precisely when varies from one population to another. The fish select special places to spawn, often close to the shore in shallow bays or over offshore sand banks. A few species, such as the American shad, migrate to rivers to spawn.

Some species of herring produce great numbers of eggs. The Atlantic herring lays 20,000 to 40,000 eggs at a time, and the American menhaden lays 500,000. The menhaden was once so common that the American Indians used the fish as fertilizer. They planted a fish with each seed put in the ground. The rotting fish fertilized the germinating plants.

The eggs of many species sink to the bed of the sea or river. They are coated with a sticky mucus, and stick to any object they happen to touch. The eggs of other species float to the surface.

In less than 2 weeks, the eggs hatch and miniature herrings emerge. Within 6 hours these may be forming shoals. They drift on the water currents, and are often carried thousands of kilometres as they grow. They are able to reproduce after 3 to 7 years.

►As a diver swims by, a predator lies in wait below a shoal of Bahamas sardines.

BONYTONGUES, ELEPHANTFISH

In a backwater of the Amazon river, a big fish stirs up the mud as it searches for worms. The arapaima's scales reflect the sunlight filtering through the murky water. A shadow falls on the arapaima as a canoe drifts towards it, the hunters with their harpoons ready. Suddenly the fish leaps out of the water as it turns to make its escape.

The arapaima is a large species of bonytongue which, along with the elephantfish, belongs to an ancient group of freshwater fish whose ancestors lived in muddy swamps more than 100 million years ago.

To look at, bonytongues and their relatives, the butterflyfish, elephantfish, featherbacks and mooneyes, are very different, but they all share one feature. Although they have teeth on their jaws, when they bite they press teeth on bones in the tongue against teeth on the roof of the mouth.

JUMPING GIANTS
Bonytongues are long narrow fish with large scales and prominent eyes. Their tails look very powerful because their fins are clustered towards the back of the body. They include one of the largest freshwater fish in the world, the Amazonian arapaima.

The arapaima and its cousin, the arawana, are both famous for making spectacular leaps out of the water,

▼▶ **Species of bonytongue and their allies** Elephantfish, *Petrocephalus catastoma* (1). Elephantfish, *Campylomormyrus rhynchophorus* (2). Adult arapaima surrounded by young (3). Young bonytongue, *Osteoglossum* species (4) at water surface. Butterflyfish (5), a popular aquarium fish. A featherback (*Notopterus chitala*) (6) followed by a freshwater hatchet fish on which it preys.

BONYTONGUES, ELEPHANTFISH Orders
Osteoglossiformes (*7 species*) and Mormyriformes (*about 106 species*)

■ ▮ ✗

🌊 Habitat: rivers, lakes and swamps.

▮ Diet: fish, insects, molluscs and other invertebrates.

Distribution: the Americas, Africa, South-east Asia, Australia.

Breeding: eggs laid in nest of plant material or on river bed. Some species show parental care, including mouth-brooding.

Size: length 6cm-4.5m; weight up to 100kg (Amazonian arapaima).

Colour: black, grey, green or gold, sometimes with brightly coloured fins.

Species mentioned in text:
Arapaima (*Arapaima gigas*)
Arawana (*Osteoglossum bicirrhosum*)
Bonytongue (*Osteoglossum* species)
Butterflyfish (*Pantodon buchholtzi*)
Elephantfish (*Petrocephalus* and *Campylomormyrus* species)
Mooneye (*Hiodon* species)

Bonytongues

Featherbacks

Butterflyfish

Elephantfish

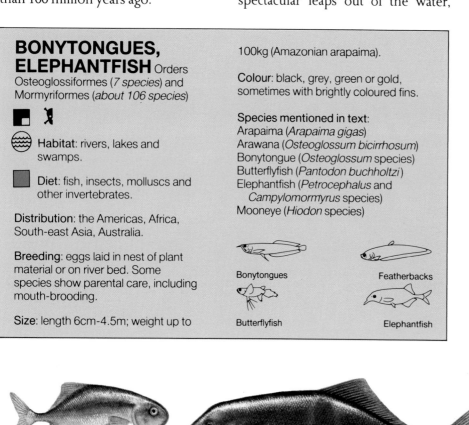

1

2

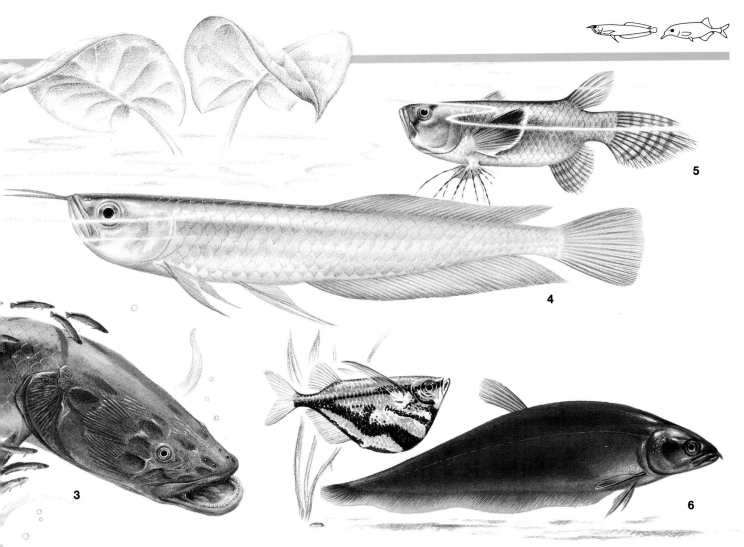

especially if cornered by fishermen. Just like their relatives in Australia, Asia and Africa, they live in shallow muddy water which often contains little oxygen. Their swimbladder is joined to their throat and acts like a lung for breathing air.

MISTAKEN FOR A BUTTERFLY
The butterflyfish of West Africa was first discovered when a butterfly collector caught one in his net. It is a small fish, only about 6 to 10cm long, and lives in grassy swamps. It swims close to the surface and feeds on floating insects. The butterflyfish will readily take to the air to catch insects or to escape from predators, using its wing-like pectoral fins to fly.

DEVOTED FATHERS
Bonytongues and butterflyfish make nests of grasses in which to care for

their eggs. The nests of the arapaima are on the river bed, but those of the butterflyfish float.

One or both parents guard the developing eggs until they hatch. The male arapaima looks after his brood for up to 3 months after they hatch, leading them to food. The young form a dense shoal around his head. Glands on the male's head appear to produce a smell or taste that attracts the young fish. The arawana and a few species of Australia and the Far East are even more protective, taking their young into their mouths if danger threatens.

ELECTRIC FISH
The mormyrid fish – elephantfish and featherbacks – hunt for worms, insects and molluscs in the muddy waters of lakes, rivers and flood pools. Like the bonytongues, many species have lung-like swimbladders and can

breathe air. Elephantfish have strange trunk-like snouts which they use to probe in the mud for food. Featherbacks are long thin fish with a long undulating fin along their back.

Many mormyrids produce weak pulses of electricity from special organs along their sides or near the tail. Special areas of the head are able to detect electrical fields as weak as 3 millionths of a billionth of an ampere. For their size, these fish have by far the largest brains of any fish. This is probably because parts of the brain are developed for receiving and for analysing electrical information. The fish sets up a weak electrical field around itself, and any object which enters this field causes a disturbance which the fish can detect. This helps the fish to find its way – and perhaps its food – in muddy water and after dark. Most mormyrids feed at night.

PIKE, SALMON, TROUT

As the water tumbles in a rush of white foam, thundering on to the rocks below, a gleaming Atlantic salmon leaps out of the water, squirming as it tries to gain enough power to clear the waterfall. The rushing water beats it back, but it tries again and again with dogged persistence until it reaches the calmer water above.

Many species of the salmon family are famous for their great migrations across oceans and up fast-flowing rivers. Together with pike and trout, they include several common fish, some of which are prized by anglers while others are important as food.

Most members of this group of fish have a small fleshy fin on their back, directly above the anal fin. They are long narrow-bodied fish, and their paired fins are set especially far back on the body. Pike, salmon and trout are carnivores – they feed on other animals. Large species feed mainly on other fish, while smaller ones eat insects, molluscs, worms and many other small invertebrates.

DANGER IN THE SHADOWS

Pike are fierce predators that lie in wait for other fish. Their bodies are long and narrow and their snouts are elongated and flattened. They have a formidable set of sharp teeth, not only on their jaws, but on the roof of their mouth as well. Their skin is greenish in colour and they have a pattern of yellowish spots that helps to conceal their outline as they skulk among the waterweeds. The dorsal, pelvic and anal fins are set far back on the body, and help to propel the fish forward rapidly once it sights its prey.

Pike live and hunt alone. Some live for many years and reach a considerable size. The largest species is the muskellunge of North America. This may be over 1.5m long and can weigh up to 30kg. It is said to catch ducks and muskrats as well as fish. Pickerel are small relatives of the pike. They seldom grow to more than 30cm long.

SLEEPING THROUGH DROUGHT

Mudminnows are tiny cousins of the pike, rarely reaching more than 15cm in length. They live in slow-flowing streams, bogs and ditches, where they lie in wait for small crustaceans and young fish. During periods of low rainfall, when their homes dry up, they burrow into the mud and sleep.

MANY GUISES, MANY NAMES

The Brown trout is a very common European fish, and has been introduced to many parts of the world for food and sport. Different populations can look and behave differently, and

▶ Large pike are often cannibals and readily make a meal of a smaller pike.

PIKE, SALMON, TROUT Order Salmoniformes
(over 300 species)

Habitat: rivers, streams, lakes, oceans at all depths; many species move from freshwater to the sea or vice versa at certain stages of their lives.

Diet: mainly invertebrates, fish.

Distribution: most cool fresh waters; oceans almost worldwide.

Breeding: usually seasonal; many species migrate to special spawning grounds. Many thousands of eggs laid in a season.

Size: length 3cm-1.5m.

Colour: mostly green, brown, grey.

Species mentioned in text:
Atlantic salmon (*Salmo salar*)
Ayu (*Plecoglossus altivelis*)
Barrel-eyes (*Opisthoproctus grimaldii*)
Brown trout (*Salmo trutta*)
Capelin (*Mallotus villosus*)
European or Northern pike (*Esox lucius*)
Muskellunge (*E. masquinongy*)
Pacific salmon (*Oncorhynchus* species)
Rainbow trout (*Salmo gairdneri*)
Sockeye salmon (*Oncorhynchus nerka*)

Pike, pickerels

Slickheads

Salmon, trout

Ayu

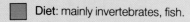

Argentines

Mudminnows

the trout also changes its appearance as it grows older. This has given rise to many names for the same species. Some trout remain in lakes throughout their lives and are called Lake trout. River trout live in rivers, and can change their colours to match the river bed. Some migrate to the sea to feed and become very silvery, thereafter being called Sea trout. These grow so well on the plentiful food in the sea that large individuals are referred to as Salmon trout.

▼Silvery shoals of Atlantic salmon were once common in the rivers of western Europe and eastern North America, but their numbers have declined as a result of overfishing and river pollution.

THE GREAT MIGRATIONS

Many salmon and trout travel to a special place to spawn. Some simply move to a shallower part of the river or lake, or even migrate from lakes to streams. Other species spend their adult lives at sea, but return to the coast or to the rivers to spawn.

The small, silvery capelin is caught in many thousands as it gathers at its favourite spawning sites in shallow coastal waters. Its close relatives, the smelts, head for the rivers. Smelts are very fatty fish. The natives of British Columbia used to catch so many migrating smelts that surplus fish, full of oils, were used as natural candles.

The greatest migrations, though, are undertaken by the salmon. Adult Pacific salmon often travel hundreds of kilometres to the mainland to breed. After this journey, they used to migrate more than 1,600km up the rivers of British Columbia to spawn, but today their way is often blocked by dams for irrigation and hydro-electric power. In some parts of the world, special fish ladders are built alongside dams to enable salmon to reach their spawning grounds. The salmon may travel 115km a day.

FATAL ATTRACTIONS

When the adult salmon reach their spawning grounds, males and females pair up. Since they left the ocean, the

▲ Salmon can leap waterfalls 3m or more high, using a flick of their powerful tail.

◄▼ At the spawning ground, a female Sockeye salmon (opposite) makes a nest in the gravel of the river bed. The large yolky eggs (second photo) are hidden in the gravel to conceal them from predators. The newly hatched salmon fry (third photo) feed on the remains of the yolk. When the yolk sac is almost exhausted (bottom photo), the fry start to feed on small invertebrates.

Male and female salmon (below) lie side by side as they spawn. The eggs and milt are shed into a hollow in the river bed dug out by the female.

males have lost their silvery shine, and have developed bright colours. Male Atlantic salmon develop blotches of red or purple, while male Pacific salmon may turn dark red. The male's jaws have become long and hooked, so they meet only at the tip. This does not matter, since the adult salmon do not feed while they are in fresh water.

The spawning grounds usually have clear water and a gravelly bed. The female salmon lays her eggs in a hollow in the gravel, known as a redd. The male sheds his sperm over them in a milky liquid called milt. Then the female moves upstream and digs another redd. As she does so, she flicks gravel over the eggs in the previous redd. This hides them from the eyes of predators and prevents them being washed away. The salmon may go on spawning for a fortnight. During this time, a female Pacific salmon may lay up to 5,000 eggs.

After spawning, Pacific salmon die. The Atlantic salmon survive to spawn again, but they are exhausted and have lost up to 40 per cent of their body weight. Many succumb to disease, and do not complete the long journey back to the sea. No salmon are known to survive more than four spawnings.

FINDING THEIR WAY

Salmon always return to the rivers of their birth to spawn, usually in the autumn. How they find their way is a mystery. They may use the position of the Sun to navigate, and perhaps the direction of the Earth's magnetic field. Ocean currents set up faint electrical fields, and the salmon may be able to detect these.

As they get nearer to home, the fish can identify the smell and taste of their home river. Each river carries its own special chemicals, washing in from the soil around it, from the under-water plants, and from fish and other animals living in the river. The salmon may even recognize the faint smell of young relatives still in the river.

▲ The Rainbow trout from North America gets its name from a band of shimmering colour that runs along its flanks. It has been introduced to other continents.

▼ A fisherman has caught a giant Pacific salmon as it journeyed to its spawning grounds. Some individuals weigh more than 45kg.

GROWN-UP NAMES

Salmon and trout go through many different stages as they grow up, and each stage has been given a name. A newly hatched salmon is called a fry or alevin. It is a tiny transparent fish only about 2cm long. By the time it has grown to about 13cm long, it has developed dark oval blotches, known as parrs, on its sides and is called a parr. These markings help camouflage the fish as it hunts.

After from 1 to 3 years, a silvery sheen develops over the parr markings, and the young salmon, now known as a smolt, is ready to migrate to the sea. Once in the sea, it grows rapidly, and after 2 years or more it is ready to return to the river to spawn.

SEEING IN THE DARK

Some relatives of salmon and trout live and breed in the deep sea. Argentines get their name from their silvery sides (*argentum* is Latin for silver). They are small fish with large eyes for seeing in the dark. Some deep-sea smelts have even larger forward-looking eyes which are set in tubes, rather like pairs of headlights. Others have tubular eyes that point upwards. They have names like spookfish or barrel-eyes.

Several of these fish have light-producing organs that glow in the dark. Bacteria in these organs perform chemical reactions that produce light. The spookfish has a flattened belly which acts as a reflector for the light it produces. The light beamed down from its belly helps to camouflage the fish when seen by predators below, which are looking up towards the brighter surface waters.

The deep-sea searsids have a novel defence. They produce a cloud of luminous particles that flash for a few seconds, giving the fish time to disappear into the darkness.

A CHANGE OF TEETH

The ayu is a strange fish that lives in the Far East. Unlike the salmon, the ayu lives as an adult in fresh water, and migrates to the sea in order to breed.

When the young fish enter the rivers, their teeth change drastically. At sea, the ayu uses cone-shaped teeth to feed on small invertebrates. In fresh water, it sheds these teeth and grows a series of comb-teeth on each jaw. Each comb has 20 to 30 fine teeth that form a kind of sieve. Inside the mouth is a group of conical teeth, which are thought to be used to scrape algae off the rocks and into the fish's mouth. The fish then closes its mouth and the water is forced out, leaving the very nutritious algae behind.

UNHELPFUL PARENTS

Unlike salmon and trout, pike do not make nest hollows. They simply shed their eggs and milt in shallow water and leave the young to fend for themselves. The eggs are quite large – 2.5-3cm across – and a big pike may lay several hundred thousand eggs a year. The pike fry start to hunt from the day they hatch.

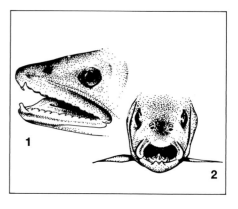

▲ The remarkable teeth of the ayu. The comb teeth (1) meet when the jaws are closed, forming a sieve. Conical teeth at the front of the mouth (2) may be used to scrape algae off rocks.

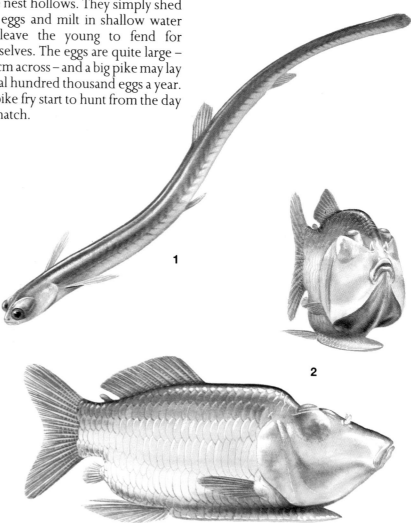

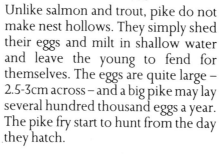

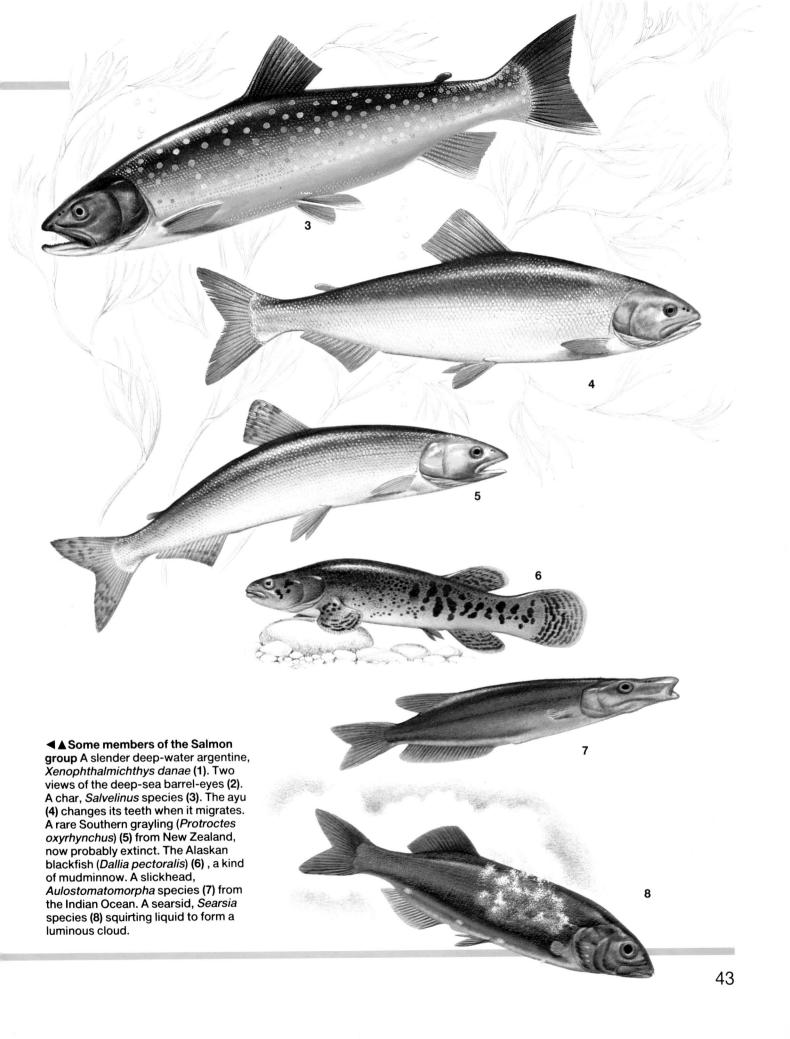

◀▲**Some members of the Salmon group** A slender deep-water argentine, *Xenophthalmichthys danae* (1). Two views of the deep-sea barrel-eyes (2). A char, *Salvelinus* species (3). The ayu (4) changes its teeth when it migrates. A rare Southern grayling (*Protroctes oxyrhynchus*) (5) from New Zealand, now probably extinct. The Alaskan blackfish (*Dallia pectoralis*) (6) , a kind of mudminnow. A slickhead, *Aulostomatomorpha* species (7) from the Indian Ocean. A searsid, *Searsia* species (8) squirting liquid to form a luminous cloud.

DRAGONFISH, LANTERNFISH

In the dimly-lit depths of the Atlantic Ocean, a fierce hunter with staring silver-rimmed eyes is stalking a small fish. A wiggling lure with a luminous red tip draws the unsuspecting fish towards the dragonfish's gaping mouth, there to be impaled on the curving dagger-sharp teeth.

▼ ► Loosejaws have no floor to their mouth – no skin or flesh stretching between the sides of the lower jaw. The jaws are very long, and the mouth can be opened extremely wide. The species shown is *Malacosteus niger*.

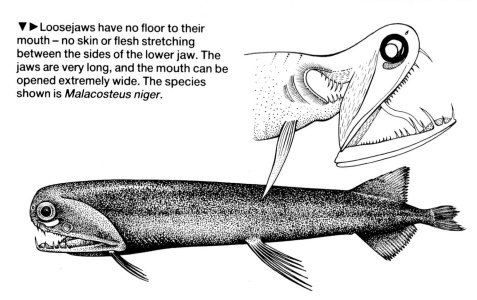

The deep sea is a rather ghostly world where the only light comes from a dim gleam in the direction of the water surface, and the coloured points of light on the bodies of luminous fish. The fish are few and far between at this depth, but altogether they make up an incredibly large number. This is because a large volume of the ocean is deep water. In fact, the average depth of the oceans is 3,790m.

For the predatory fish, meals are a rare and unpredictable occurrence, but they have ways of making the most of any opportunity. Many have large eyes adapted for seeing in dim light. Some have huge gaping jaws that can seize prey as large as themselves. Others rely on luring their prey to them. Since attractive colours are of little use in semi-darkness, the fish use luminous (glowing) lures instead.

Some equally bizarre adaptations help to protect the smaller predators from the larger ones. Silver sides that mirror the blackness of the ocean and patterns of many luminous spots that confuse their outlines are among the disguises used.

FEARSOME PREDATORS

Viperfish are some of the fiercest predators of the oceans. Their mouths are armed with long sharp teeth that curve backwards so that their prey cannot escape. The front teeth of the upper jaw point forwards and are used to stab their victims. Still more flexible teeth in the throat help to grip the prey and push it gradually down the throat to the stomach.

Many viperfish are less than 30cm long, but some reach a length of 60cm or more. However, a viperfish is able to swallow a fish of its own size or larger. Its powerful jaws can be separated to make a large mouth. Also, the bones of the neck are made of flexible cartilage so that it can throw its head back to open the jaws yet more.

As the fish opens its mouth to seize its prey, it draws its heart and gills deeper into its body, safely out of the way of the struggling prey. Its stomach is extremely elastic, and can stretch around large prey.

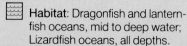

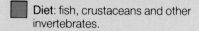

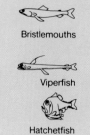

These fish stay in deep water from 1,500 to 2,500m down by day, and move up to about 450m to hunt at night. Their large silver-rimmed eyes are up to 30 times more sensitive to dim light than human eyes. Rows of tiny light-producing organs pick out the viperfish's shape, giving off a strange blue-green light.

TELESCOPIC EYES
The deep-sea hatchetfish has bulging tubular eyes with yellow lenses that are directed upwards. They act rather like binoculars, giving the fish good vision in the dim light. The hatchet-fish, which is only about 8cm long, feeds on small crustaceans. It can see their silhouettes outlined against the

◄The head of a viperfish, a vicious deep-sea predator with sharply pointed teeth. The silvery background to its eye is a reflector which helps it to see in dim light. Organs that produce light inside its mouth help to lure fish to their death.

▼This deep-sea hatchetfish, genus *Argyropelecus*, looks fat from the side, but thin when seen from in front.

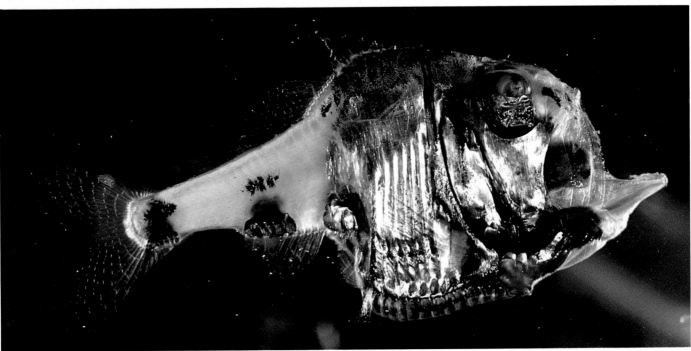

faint glow of light coming down from the surface. To prevent its own predators detecting it in the same way, it has some light-producing organs on its belly which conceal its shadow. Its mirror-like sides reflect the colour of the dark water around it, so it is almost invisible when viewed from the side.

DRAGONS OF THE DEEP

Although they rarely grow longer than 30cm, deep-sea dragonfish are fierce predators. They have slender dark bodies covered in large scales, and a large head armed with long curved teeth. Their mouths open so wide that they probably cannot be closed completely. To catch its prey, the dragonfish has a long lure on its chin, with a swollen luminous tip. In some species of dragonfish, the lure may be five times longer than the fish itself. Nobody knows how it is used.

BRISTLEMOUTHS

Bristlemouths probably comprise the world's most numerous fish – they occur in even greater numbers than herrings. They live in fairly deep water in all the world's oceans, and tens of thousands can be caught at a time in trawl nets.

Bristlemouths get their name from their fine bristle-like teeth. They are tiny fish – many are no more than 6cm long – and they feed on small crustaceans and other invertebrates. Many larger fish depend upon them as their most important food, and they could one day supply the human population as well, in the form of protein-rich fish paste.

◀ With its large teeth and glowing (luminous) chin lures, this deep-sea hunter displays the typical features of scaled dragonfish.

▼ Decorated with lights – a deep-sea viperfish photographed under ultraviolet light shows a brilliant pattern of organs that produce light. Its widely spread (gaping) mouth and long teeth show it to be a fierce predator.

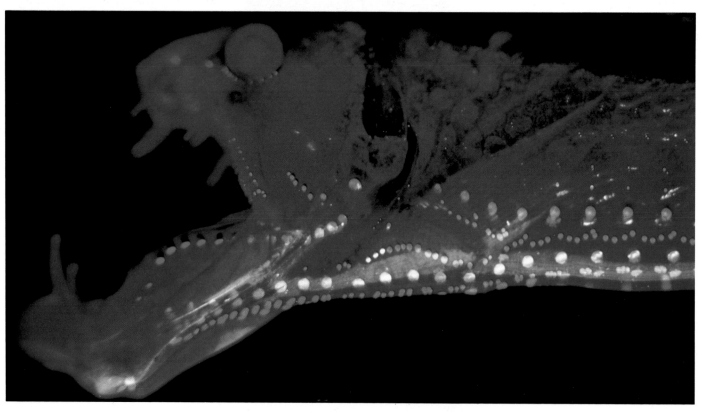

GIANT TAILS

Giant tails, or giganturids, are strange eel-like fish. They have smooth scaleless skin, a large mouth, savage teeth, and a tail fin that is drawn out into a long thin filament. Giant tails have extraordinary forward-pointing tubular eyes at the sides of their heads, rather like the headlamps of some racing cars. This gives them very good vision for hunting their prey. Many of the fish they catch are luminous, so the giganturid's mouth and stomach have a thick black lining to hide the light emitted from its last meal.

LIVING LANTERNS

Many deep-sea fish have light organs – tiny patches of skin that give off light, usually in the form of a bluish-green glow. Sometimes the scales overlying the light organs form lenses to concentrate the light. There may also be silvery reflectors behind the light organs or coloured skin in front for further effect. The light is produced by special chemical reactions. Often the light organs are arranged in long, parallel rows along the fish's body, like pearly buttons.

In many fish the amount of light given off is controlled by the fish's nervous system. In several deep-sea fish, each eye can detect how much light is reaching it from the surface waters, and adjust the fish's own light output to match.

OCEAN CAMOUFLAGE

In these dimly lit waters, there is still a faint glow of light coming down from the surface, so each fish casts a shadow on the water below. This gives away its presence to any predator lurking

► The string of beads on the underside of this bristlemouth are its light organs. Each species has its own distinctive pattern, and males and females often have slightly different patterns, too.

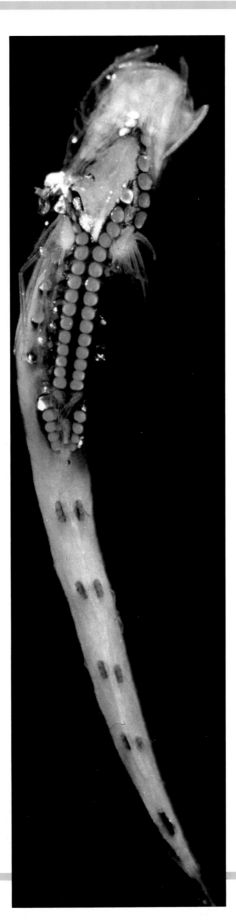

below. There is not enough light for pale colours to be of any use in camouflaging the shadow, but light organs serve the same purpose.

Silvery mirror sides reflect the exact colour and brightness of the water around, so giving perfect camouflage at any time of day.

LIGHTS FOR SHOW

Not all light organs are for camouflage. In many dragonfish and viperfish, tiny light organs occur in distinct patterns along the fish's outline – on its upper and lower edges and fins. These may be used by the fish to recognize members of their own species, or to find mates. They could also be used by the fish to space themselves out, so that they are not hunting too close to each other. Some deep-sea fish have large bright light organs under their eyes. These may be used like headlamps to find their prey.

BRAVE DECOY

Male lanternfish have a very bright light organ on their back close to the tail. Females do not have this light. One of the main enemies of lanternfish are tunas. Tuna fishermen in the Pacific were puzzled because when they examined the tuna they caught, the tunas' stomachs contained mainly male lanternfish. Most of the lanternfish they caught in their nets, though, were females.

It may be that when they are set upon by tunas, the male lanternfish dart away, flashing the tail lights and diverting the attention of the tuna from the females. The females stay put and in theory should escape the tuna. However, instead they get trapped in the fishermen's nets. Thus the male lanternfish's sacrifice is wasted.

LURED BY THE LIGHT

Some deep-sea fish use lights to lure their prey. Dragonfish have fleshy luminous growths on their chins and these may act as a lure. If another fish comes close to the lure, they start viciously snapping and biting at it. The lure may also be used to sense vibrations in the water to warn the fish of approaching prey. The viperfish has a lure on the tip of its dorsal fin instead. It can swing it round in front of the mouth when necessary.

Animals that use lures to entice their prey risk having the lure damaged by hungry prey. The viperfish has light organs inside its mouth as well, so its prey is led closer and closer to its unsuspected and certain death.

SEA LIZARDS

In warm shallow seas the world over live small lizard-like fish that waddle over the seabed, using their pelvic fins like stubby little legs. Lizardfish are often overlooked because they are usually well camouflaged. They spend much of their time propped up on their fins, waiting for small fish and shrimps to swim within reach. Then they dart out very quickly, just as lizards dart after their prey. Their speed is due to their tail fins, and as they move they spread their pectoral fins rather like wings. The lizardfish leap on their prey and swallow them whole. The most famous lizardfish is a species of Bombay duck from the delta of the River Ganges, which is eaten dried and salted as a delicacy.

LIVING TRIPODS

The tripodfish are kinds of lizardfish that live on the floor of the deep sea, sometimes as deep as 6,000m. Their tail fins have a long stiff lower lobe and the pelvic fins are also stiff, so the fish have a natural tripod to prop them up on the bottom. This enables them to search for food in the clearer water above the muddy seabed.

Sometimes tripodfish walk on these stilts. At other times they leap along rather like little frogs, using the tripod to land on. The pectoral fins are also very long and fine, and these may be used to sense vibrations in the water.

Tripodfish's eyes are very small, and the water where they live is very dark, so they need to use other senses to find their food.

REPRODUCTION AT DEPTH

Very little detail is known about the reproduction of many of these deep-sea fish. Bristlemouth eggs have been found floating in the ocean, and they hatched into tiny larvae rather like sardines. The luminous organs did not appear until after the larvae had changed into adults.

MINIATURE MALES

One of the strangest of stories is that of the Stalk-eye dragonfish. This has weird larvae with eyes on very long stalks (up to one-third of the body length) at the side of the head. The eyes can swivel to look in different directions. They also have transparent bodies, and their intestines are so long that the rear part of them hangs out of the body. As the larvae grow, the eye-stalks gradually become shorter, and so do their intestines.

Male and female of the Stalk-eye dragonfish develop rather differently. The female becomes black, and grows pelvic fins, rows of light organs, and luminous chin lures and powerful jaws with curved teeth. The male, however, is brown, and has no pelvic fins, lure or teeth. Instead, he has a large light organ just below his eye. He does not feed or grow once he becomes adult, so he remains less than 5cm long. The female, though, is an active predator, and may reach a length of over 30cm.

▼This is not a lizard hiding among heather, but a lizardfish, genus *Synodus*, among corals on the Great Barrier Reef of Australia.

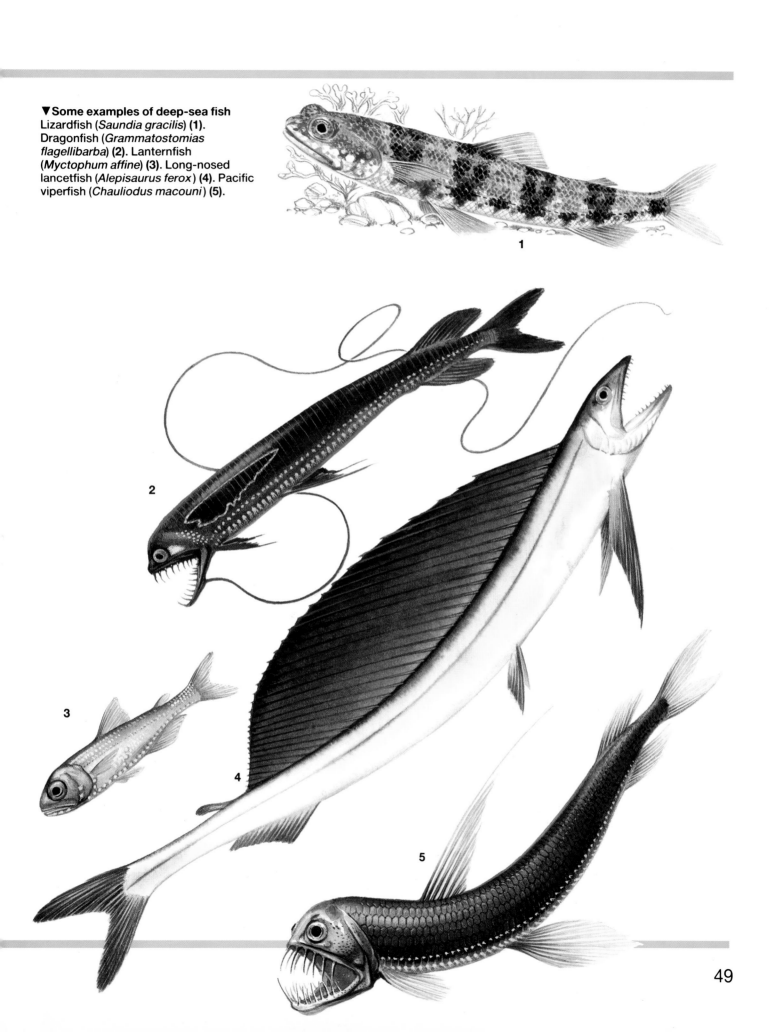

▼**Some examples of deep-sea fish**
Lizardfish (*Saundia gracilis*) **(1)**.
Dragonfish (*Grammatostomias flagellibarba*) **(2)**. Lanternfish (*Myctophum affine*) **(3)**. Long-nosed lancetfish (*Alepisaurus ferox*) **(4)**. Pacific viperfish (*Chauliodus macouni*) **(5)**.

TOADFISH, ANGLERFISH

A small fish hovers over the coral reef, searching for food. As it passes a seaweed-covered rock, it spots a fleshy worm that wriggles enticingly. The fish draws closer to investigate, unaware that it is being watched by a pair of eyes in the "rock". As the fish prepares to take the bait, the anglerfish suddenly opens its huge mouth and the little fish is sucked in.

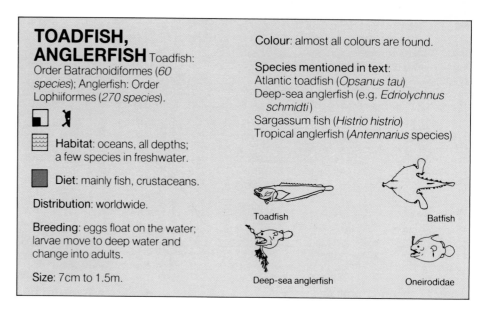

TOADFISH, ANGLERFISH Toadfish: Order Batrachoidiformes (*60 species*); Anglerfish: Order Lophiiformes (*270 species*).

Habitat: oceans, all depths; a few species in freshwater.

Diet: mainly fish, crustaceans.

Distribution: worldwide.

Breeding: eggs float on the water; larvae move to deep water and change into adults.

Size: 7cm to 1.5m.

Colour: almost all colours are found.

Species mentioned in text:
Atlantic toadfish (*Opsanus tau*)
Deep-sea anglerfish (e.g. *Edriolychnus schmidti*)
Sargassum fish (*Histrio histrio*)
Tropical anglerfish (*Antennarius* species)

Toadfish

Batfish

Deep-sea anglerfish

Oneirodidae

Toadfish, frogfish and anglerfish are some of the laziest predators in the oceans. They are well camouflaged; some are even covered in little flaps of skin to look like a rock coated in small pieces of seaweed. Some of the anglerfish that live on coral reefs may be brilliantly coloured, but they are easily mistaken for sponges or sea squirts. They wait for their prey to come within reach, then open their huge mouths. Water rushes in, and the prey is swept in with it. Other anglerfish go one step further than this. A fleshy lure or "bait" is wiggled in front of the mouth to draw the prey closer.

FISH THAT CROAK

Toadfish live at the bottom of clear temperate and tropical seas, buried in the sand or hidden among seaweeds. They have broad toad-like heads with bulging eyes, very large mouths and lots of small sharp teeth. Their pelvic fins are stiff and muscular, like stubby little legs, and toadfish can hop across the sea floor in much the same way that toads move. When its prey – a small fish or shrimp – comes within reach, a toadfish will leap on it, snapping its huge jaws tight shut.

The resemblance to toads does not stop here: toadfish can actually croak. They each have a heart-shaped swim-bladder that is used to amplify the sound. The resulting sounds are loud enough to be heard out of water. Underwater they can be deafening – from 60cm away the volume can be 100 decibels, equivalent to the sound of a railway train. As well as these loud blasts, each toadfish also produces quieter grunts and growls.

The sounds are probably used by the toadfish to defend its territory. It guards fiercely the area of the seabed in which it hunts. If another fish approaches, this will provoke a whole series of grunts and blasts, accompanied by threatening postures. After mating, male toadfish are left to guard the eggs. They will croak loudly if their eggs are threatened.

TROUBLE WITH TOADS

The toadfish's disguise can prove a problem to divers and swimmers. It is easy to step on a toadfish by accident. This can be an unpleasant experience, because the toadfish has sharp hollow spines on its dorsal fin and gill covers, which inject venom when touched. The wound is extremely painful, but is not known to be fatal.

▶Toadfish are sluggish predators that rely on their camouflage in catching their prey. This species, from the Atlantic Ocean, has a voice like a foghorn.

◀A tropical anglerfish wiggles its fleshy lure to attract small fish to come within reach of its large mouth. When it opens its mouth, the prey will be sucked in.

SKILFUL FISHERMEN

In most anglerfish, the first dorsal fin ray has become a long flexible lure for attracting prey. This ray is often separated from the rest of the fin and set well forward on the snout, so as to lure the prey towards the angler's large mouth. A small flap of skin at the tip of the lure can look very like a small fish when it is wiggled rapidly.

Some anglerfish can bend their lure down almost in front of their mouths as the prey comes closer. They must be sure to open their mouths quickly and suck in the prey before it has time to take a bite at the lure.

A WORLD OF CAMOUFLAGE

Far out in the Atlantic Ocean is the Sargasso Sea, named after the many large clumps of a floating seaweed called sargassum weed. Many of the creatures that live in the sargassum weed are camouflaged to match it. Crabs, shrimps, sea slugs and fish are all coloured greenish-brown, mottled with yellow like the weed. Survival is a tricky business where both predator and prey are camouflaged.

The master of camouflage is the Sargassum fish, a small frogfish. Not only does its colour match the sargassum weed, but its body shape looks like the irregular outlines of the seaweed. The rays of its fins sometimes end in round swellings that resemble the air bladders of sargassum weed. The fish's pectoral and pelvic fins are muscular, like little legs. It climbs about in the weed, creeping up on its prey, mainly crustaceans and small fish, including other Sargassum fish.

DANGER IN THE DEEP

Deep-sea anglerfish all look much like miniature sea monsters, with gaping mouths, long curving fangs and weird

▼This female deep-sea anglerfish has two parasitic male anglerfish fused to her body. They will spend the rest of their lives with her.

▲Species of anglerfish Deep-sea anglerfish can look quite unusual. A female anglerfish, *Edriolynchus* species (1) with three parasitic male anglerfish attached. The Black anglerfish, *Melanocoetus* species (2) has an elastic stomach, and can swallow prey that is larger than itself. This deep-sea anglerfish, *Linophryne* species, (3) has glowing (luminous) chin barbels as well as a luminous lure.

shapes. Most have very smooth dark brown or black bodies, with no scales, but some have bony lumps or spines in their skins.

In deep water, very little light penetrates, so ordinary lures would be no real use. The lures of many deep-sea anglers have luminous tips. Often the tip of the lure is swollen, and contains bacteria that produce light by various chemical reactions. The lures flash yellowish-green or blue as the anglerfish hunts. Certain deep-sea species have very long lures than can be held out a long way in front of the mouth. These are slowly drawn in as the prey comes closer.

FISHING IN THE DARK

The prey may be able to see the lure, but how does the anglerfish see its prey? Many deep-sea anglerfish have poor eyesight, and probably use smell and touch to detect their prey. The lateral line system along their sides can sense slight vibrations in the water that might be made by a passing fish.

Some anglerfish have luminous barbels (fleshy tentacles) on their chins. These barbels may be branched like tufts of seaweed with luminous tips. The light in these barbels is produced not by bacteria, but by the fish's own

chemical reactions. The purpose of these barbels is not clear. They may be used for touch and taste, or they may act as extra lures.

A TENDER TRAP

A deep-sea anglerfish that goes by the rather long Latin name of *Thaumatichthys* has an almost foolproof way of luring fish right into its mouth. Its two-pronged lure actually hangs from the roof of its mouth. It swims along or lies in wait with its mouth wide open to display the lure. The prey swims up to the lure until it is right inside the anglerfish's mouth. Then the angler gently and tightly closes its jaws around it.

WALKING BATFISH

Batfish live in warm shallow seas. Their large pectoral fins spread out like bat wings, and their pelvic fins are used like legs for walking over the sandy seabed. When they find a good spot to wait for prey, they dig into the sand backwards, until only their front end protrudes, propped up on the pelvic fins. Then they wiggle their lures hopefully. Some batfish have long pointed snouts and look almost triangular when viewed from above. Others have a rounded outline.

LONG RIBBONS OF EGGS

Several anglerfish of coastal waters move to deeper water in spring to spawn. They produce large numbers of eggs in a long ribbon-like mass of jelly as much as 9m long. The newly hatched young move to the surface, where they feed on plankton for a time before settling on the seabed.

DOMINATING FEMALES

A female deep-sea anglerfish may be 20 times larger than the male. Spawning takes place in deep water, but the eggs float to the surface. Huge numbers of eggs are produced – up to 5 million at a time – by some species.

Distinct male and female larvae hatch from the eggs. Each female has a small knob on her snout which will grow into a lure. The male has no such structure. As they grow bigger, the larvae move to deeper water. After about 2 months, a very rapid change of form takes place, and they turn into young adults.

The females will take many years to reach maturity, but males already have well-developed sex organs and are capable of mating. But their jaws are weak and shaped rather like pincers, and they grow only slowly. They will use their pincer-like jaws to grip the skin of the female during mating.

MATES FOR LIFE

In some deep-sea anglerfish species, the males do not feed as adults. In order to survive, they must find a mate quickly. Once a male finds a female, he clings to her and gradually his flesh becomes fused with hers. Then he feeds directly from her blood. Most of his body organs are absorbed, but the sex organs continue to grow. When he is mature, he will release his sperm directly into the female's blood.

◀Two species of batfish *Halieutichthys aculeatus* (1); *Ogcocephalus parvus* (2). Batfish shuffle over the seabed on their pelvic fins.

CARP, CATFISH

CARP, CATFISH

Carp: Order Cypriniformes (*2,500 species*); catfish: Siluriformes (*2,000 species*); characins: Characiformes (*2,200 species*); milkfish: Gonorhynchiformes (*30 species*).

 Habitat: mostly fresh water.

Diet: fish, invertebrates, algae.

Distribution: worldwide.

Breeding: lay up to 1 million eggs on mud or sand, leaves, or in nest. Parental care and mouth-brooding in some catfish and characins.

Size: length 13mm (catfish) to 2.5m (Electric eel).

Colour: almost all colours occur.

Species mentioned in text:
Barber eel (*Plotosus lineatus*)
Bitterling (*Rhodeus sericeus*)
Bleeding heart tetra (*Hyphessobrycon rubrostigma*)
Carp (*Cyprinus carpio*)
Crucian carp (*Carassius carassius*)
Eel-tail catfish (*Neosilurus* and *Tandanus* species)
Electric catfish (*Malapterurus electricus*)
Electric eel (*Electrophorus electricus*)
Freshwater hatchetfish (*Carnegiella* species)
Gafftopsail catfish (*Bagre marinus*)
Glass catfish (*Kryptopterus bicirrhus*)
Goldfish (*Carassius auratus*)
Splashing tetra (*Copella arnoldi*)
Upside-down catfish (*Synodontis nigriventris*)

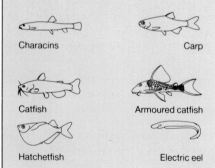

Characins   Carp

Catfish   Armoured catfish

Hatchetfish   Electric eel

With a loud splash, a carp breaks the surface of the murky water to reach the air. Ripples spread outwards in ever-increasing circles. Its need for oxygen satisfied, the carp returns to its supper, lazily searching among the weeds for any small edible morsels, alive or dead.

Carp and catfish make up an important group of fish which includes about four-fifths of all the world's freshwater fish. They are very varied in shape and habits, ranging from fierce Amazonian piranhas to electric catfish, delicate tetras, goldfish and swordtails.

Most have a prominent dorsal fin, well separated pelvic and anal fins, and a forked tail fin. Characins and catfish often have a second, fleshy, dorsal fin near the tail, and some catfish have a long anal fin running almost the whole length of the belly.

THE LISTENING FISH

These fish have a very special way of hearing under water. Sound waves passing through the water are picked up by the swimbladder, which is connected to each fish's ears by a series of levers formed by some of the spinal bones. These levers make the vibrations greater as they are transmitted to the ears. This arrangement

▲The carp (in front) has been farmed for centuries in Europe. The Crucian carp from Asia is related to the goldfish.

▼The markings on the dorsal fin of this Bleeding heart tetra may help to keep shoals together in dark water.

probably gives the fish extra good hearing, which is particularly useful in the muddy water where many of these species live.

A TASTE FOR BLOOD

The piranhas of South America are some of the fiercest fish in the world. Although most species are little more than 30cm long, they can attack and kill animals much larger than themselves, literally tearing them to pieces. The smell of blood will attract many hundreds of piranhas in a remarkably short time. Piranhas seem to feed in a frenzy. Each fish darts in and bites off a chunk of flesh. In the confusion, some piranhas may get eaten by others. Piranhas normally feed on fish.

THE CAT'S WHISKERS

Catfish get their name from the fleshy whiskers (barbels) on their snouts. The barbels are used for smelling, tasting and touching. Many catfish live in rather slow-moving muddy water, where smell and touch are more important than sight for finding food. They have broad heads, large mouths

▲ Goldfish have been specially bred for centuries, and many of the ornamental varieties could not survive in the wild.

◀ The piranha (genus *Serrasalmus*) has short teeth with sharp edges. Although feared for its attacks on humans, its normal diet is wounded fish.

on the underside of their snouts, and small eyes. Many catfish are naked, with no scales, while the armoured catfish of South America have rows of large bony plates up to 3mm thick for protection. The smallest catfish are less than 13mm long. The largest species may reach a length of 3m.

Most catfish feed near the bottom of lakes and rivers, sucking up worms and other small invertebrates. The largest species eat fish. A few species have thin comb-like teeth for scraping at algae on rocks. Catfish feed mainly at night, hiding by day under stones and logs. Some species are important food fish, especially in South America and India.

DEFENSIVE MECHANISMS

For small fish, armour would slow down their movements and make escape impossible. The Glass catfish of Asia is only 10cm long, but it has a novel defence. It is quite transparent – you can see its internal organs, and even the leaves of waterweeds behind it. When the light catches its body, it reflects shimmering rainbow colours. The fish's invisible outline and the flash of colour confuse predators.

Other catfish have more vicious defences. The madtoms of North America (genus *Noturus*) and the eel-tail catfish of the Indian and Pacific oceans have poison glands at the bases of their spiny fins. The larger eel-tail catfish, up to 1m long, inflict wounds that are slow to heal, and are said to be able to kill larger animals. They have bright yellow stripes to warn attackers of the danger.

IN FOR A SHOCK

Some fish use electric shocks to stun their prey. The Electric catfish, up to 1m long, can produce shocks of up to 450 volts. The electricity is produced by living batteries along the fish's body. The Electric eel (not really an eel but a catfish), which grows to 2.5m in length, similarly can generate 600 volts, enough to give an adult person a severe shock. This fish also uses its electricity to navigate. It sends out tiny short pulses of electricity to produce an electric field around itself. Objects moving in the water nearby disturb the electric field. In the muddy water, sight is of little use, and the eyes of the adult fish are tiny.

A MOUTHFUL OF BABIES

Catfish make good parents. When they spawn in spring and summer, the male makes a nest in the sand or mud, sometimes surrounding it with a wall of weed. The female lays her eggs in the nest, then the male fertilizes them. The male, or maybe both parents, then stays to guard the eggs and young until they are big and strong enough to survive on their own.

Some of the sea catfish lay the biggest eggs of any bony fish. The eggs of the Gafftopsail catfish are 2.5cm in diameter. The male keeps up to 50 eggs in his mouth for safety, starving

▲ This crucifix fish gets its name from the crucifix-like shape of bones in the underside of its skull.

◄These young Barber eels (a kind of eel-tail catfish), with poisonous fin spines, have warning colours.

▲During the rainy season, many catfish move into flooded plains to feed or breed. These catfish in Tanzania became trapped when the dry season arrived.

▼A catfish crosses the road. This Indian species has lung-like organs which allows it to breathe air. It uses its pectoral fins for crawling.

himself until the eggs hatch and the young fish are a month old. By this time he has not eaten for 8 weeks.

WALKING TALKING FISH
Many catfish live in shallow muddy water which gets short of oxygen in warm weather. Several species are able to use air for breathing. Some use their swimbladders like a lung. Others have specially adapted gill chambers for absorbing extra oxygen.

Catfish of the family Clariidae can all breathe air and travel over land by wiggling their bodies like a snake and shuffling on their stiff pectoral fins. If their pool dries up, they can move away in search of another. As a last resort, they bury themselves in the mud and survive rather like lungfish until the pool fills with water again.

The swimbladder may also be used as a resonating chamber for making croaking and grunting sounds.

FLYING HATCHETFISH
The hatchetfish of South America use their pectoral fins like wings. They can leap up to 90cm into the air and glide over the water, flapping their "wings" so fast that they make a buzzing noise. Hatchetfish often skim along the surface for some distance with their tail

and chests dipping in the water before they get up enough speed to take off. They live in streams, where they feed on insects at the surface, and probably leap into the air to escape from their predators.

THE FOOD OF EMPERORS
Carp have been farmed for some hundreds, if not thousands, of years in China. They are good to eat, and easy to feed, as they will eat almost everything, from algae, molluscs and other invertebrates, to cheese sandwiches and sausages. They will even eat dead plant and animal material. Loaches are often kept in aquaria to keep the bottom clean. Rasboras, on the other hand, feed at the water surface, catching insects that fly just above the water. They are capable of jumping out of aquaria.

Carp with beautiful colours, mirror scales and many different fin shapes have been bred, including the goldfish. Carp have no teeth on their jaws, but use teeth in their throats to chew up plant material. Many have barbels for finding their food.

Some carp, and their close relatives, the loaches and suckers, have large sucker-like mouths for feeding on the bottom. The hillstream loaches live in fast-flowing rivers throughout much of Asia. Their pectoral and pelvic fins are rounded and often joined to form a true sucker, which the fish all use for anchoring themselves firmly to the bottom or to rocks.

WEATHERFISH
Like many other loaches, the European and Oriental weatherfish are sensitive to changes in atmospheric pressure. This is probably because of their highly developed swimbladder, which is used like a lung in stagnant water. If the atmospheric pressure falls sharply, as it does just before a thunderstorm, the fish get agitated and let out air. People sometimes use them as living barometers.

SAFETY IN NUMBERS
Carp and minnows are not very good parents. Most species simply scatter their eggs in shallow water as they swim. A few species stick their eggs to water plants. After that, the eggs and young are on their own. But a female carp may lay over a million eggs in a season, so she can afford to lose 999,999 of them. Goldfish and some other carp can live 40 years, which makes for an enormous total of eggs.

In contrast, tetras lay their many eggs on leaves overhanging the water, where they are out of reach of predators. Each male and female pair leaps out of the water and attach themselves to the underside of a leaf, belly uppermost. There they lay and fertilize a few eggs before falling back into the water. This is repeated many times. The male returns to the site about every half an hour to splash water over the eggs with his tail to keep them moist. When the eggs hatch a few weeks later, the young fish fall into the water.

A BORROWED NURSERY
The bitterling lays her eggs inside a freshwater mussel. She nudges the mussel to make it open, then slips her long egg-laying tube between the mussel's shells. The male sheds his milt (sperms) nearby, and this is then drawn into the mussel as it feeds. When the eggs hatch, the larvae cling to the mussel's gills until they are big enough to swim. Then they escape. The mussel also benefits from this arrangement. It spawns at the same time as the bitterling, and its larvae are carried away on the bitterling's gills to find new homes.

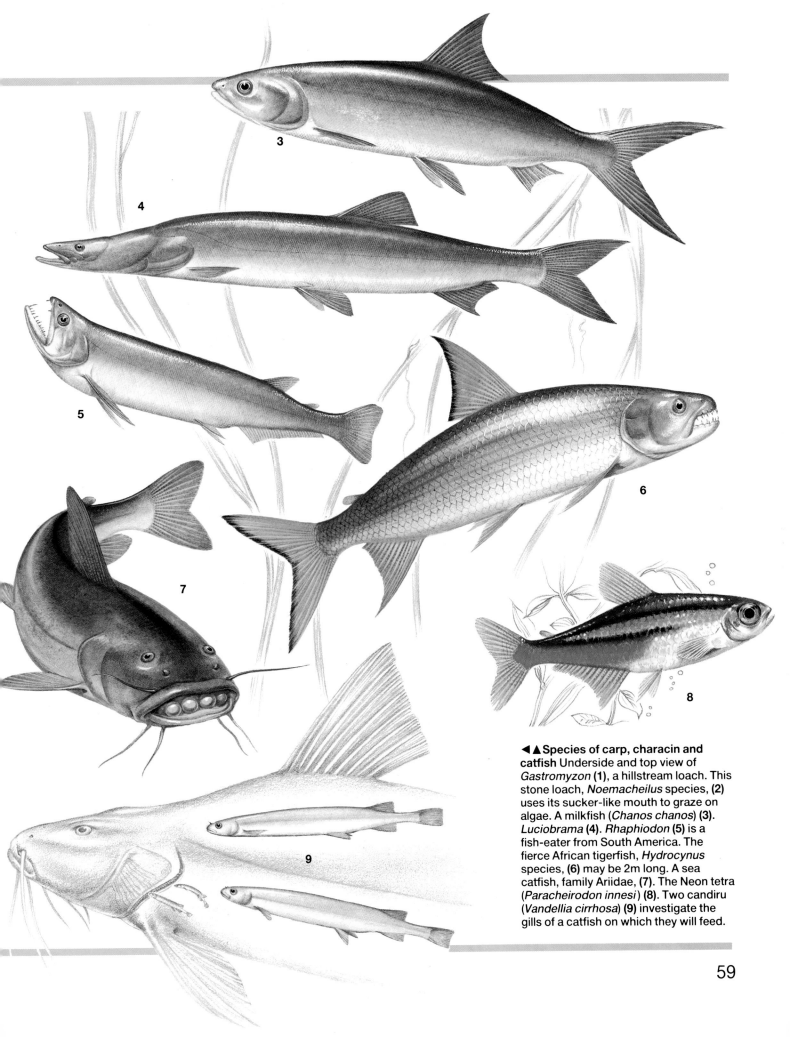

◀▲**Species of carp, characin and catfish** Underside and top view of *Gastromyzon* **(1)**, a hillstream loach. This stone loach, *Noemacheilus* species, **(2)** uses its sucker-like mouth to graze on algae. A milkfish (*Chanos chanos*) **(3)**. *Luciobrama* **(4)**. *Rhaphiodon* **(5)** is a fish-eater from South America. The fierce African tigerfish, *Hydrocynus* species, **(6)** may be 2m long. A sea catfish, family Ariidae, **(7)**. The Neon tetra (*Paracheirodon innesi*) **(8)**. Two candiru (*Vandellia cirrhosa*) **(9)** investigate the gills of a catfish on which they will feed.

59

COD

In the greenish-blue light near the seabed, a dense shoal of cod begins to stir. As the light fades, the fish start to move apart, revealing their pale bellies. They swim slowly over the mud, rippling their large dorsal fins as they tilt and turn in search of fish, squid and other invertebrates.

The cod family contains some of the most familiar food fish, such as cod, haddock, whiting and hake. These are medium-sized fish, 60 to 100cm long. Once the cod fishery was so important that 400 million fish were caught each year in the North Atlantic alone, but overfishing has since drastically reduced catches. Cod weighing up to 90kg used to be caught, but today an 18kg cod is considered a giant.

ALONG COASTS OR IN POOLS

Cod feed mainly on other fish, but the smaller species also prey on crustaceans and other invertebrates. Most cod live in shallow waters. A few species, though, are found in the deeper waters beyond the continental shelves. Generally, cod spend the day in large shoals near the bottom and spread out at night to feed. Only one species, the burbot, spends its whole

life in fresh water. It is found in deep cold lakes and streams throughout much of the Northern Hemisphere.

Cod have rather soft, spineless fins. In some species the dorsal fin is divided into two or three parts, and the anal fin may also be in two parts. In others, dorsal and anal fins extend for much of the body, and may join with the tail fin. Most cod have a single whisker-like projection (barbel) on their chins to help them feel and smell for food. The rocklings, small eel-like fish that live in rock pools, have four more barbels on their snouts.

▲ Poor cod are found in large numbers near the shores of Europe, especially near rocks. They feed mainly on shrimps and small squid.

STRANGE SHELTERS

Pearlfish are small cod that live in most unusual homes. Some live inside sea cucumbers (relatives of starfish), while others live in cushion stars or in the mantle cavities of oysters (hence the name pearlfish). A pearlfish will enter the sea cucumber backwards, inserting the tip of its pointed tail, and then wriggling in. Some pearlfish simply use the cucumbers as shelters, leaving them to hunt for food. Others feed on the cucumbers' insides.

EGGS APLENTY

Cod are some of the most prolific spawners of all fish. A female ling (genus *Molva*), which grows to 1.5m long, may produce up to 28,360,000 eggs at a time, a record broken only by the Ocean sunfish. The Atlantic cod lays up to 9 million eggs at a time. The eggs float to the surface of the ocean, where they are scattered by the currents and the wind. Most never hatch: many are eaten by adult fish, others by various invertebrates.

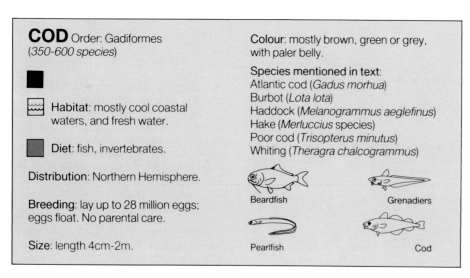

COD Order: Gadiformes
(350-600 species)

■

〰 Habitat: mostly cool coastal waters, and fresh water.

■ Diet: fish, invertebrates.

Distribution: Northern Hemisphere.

Breeding: lay up to 28 million eggs; eggs float. No parental care.

Size: length 4cm-2m.

Colour: mostly brown, green or grey, with paler belly.

Species mentioned in text:
Atlantic cod (*Gadus morhua*)
Burbot (*Lota lota*)
Haddock (*Melanogrammus aeglefinus*)
Hake (*Merluccius* species)
Poor cod (*Trisopterus minutus*)
Whiting (*Theragra chalcogrammus*)

Beardfish   Grenadiers

Pearlfish   Cod

The eggs are small, and contain very little yolk, so the young larvae have to start feeding as soon as they hatch. Often cod eggs contain oil droplets, which help them to float in the plankton. Here the young fry feed on even smaller plankton animals until they are strong enough to swim. Then they move to shallow water. When they are about 2 months old and 2.5cm long, they move to the bottom to live as adults.

Numerous cod migrate to special spawning grounds, where the eggs and milt are shed. The North Atlantic hake, for example, begins spawning in spring in water deeper than 180m. As the season progresses, however, it migrates to shallower water. The fertilized eggs float at the surface and the future hake population is dependent on the weather. If the wind blows the eggs away from the rich inshore feeding grounds, very few of the young survive. This leads to a failure of the hake fishing industry a few years later.

DEEP-SEA RAT-TAILS

The rat-tails, or grenadiers, are some of the only bottom-living deep-sea fish to have organs that produce light. They have whip-like tails with no tail fins. Their large heads are covered in heavy armour, and their eyes are very large for seeing in dim light. Rat-tails

also communicate by sound. The male uses his swimbladder to create a drumming noise, and also makes clicking sounds. The mouth of a rat-tail is on the underside of the snout, for feeding on the bottom. The snout may protrude in front of the mouth, which is useful for probing the mud and sand.

Although rarely seen, rat-tails are probably even more numerous than cod. There is a huge volume of ocean below 200m, far greater than the volume of shallow water over the continental shelves. Rat-tails may well inhabit most of this unexplored sea world. The majority of species rarely reach more than 50cm in length, but one or two grow to 80cm.

▲Rat-tails, or grenadiers, are found all over the world in deep water. Males make a drumming noise for communicating in the dark.

▼Two species of cod The Atlantic cod (1) and the haddock (2). These are two of the world's most important fish caught by commercial fishermen.

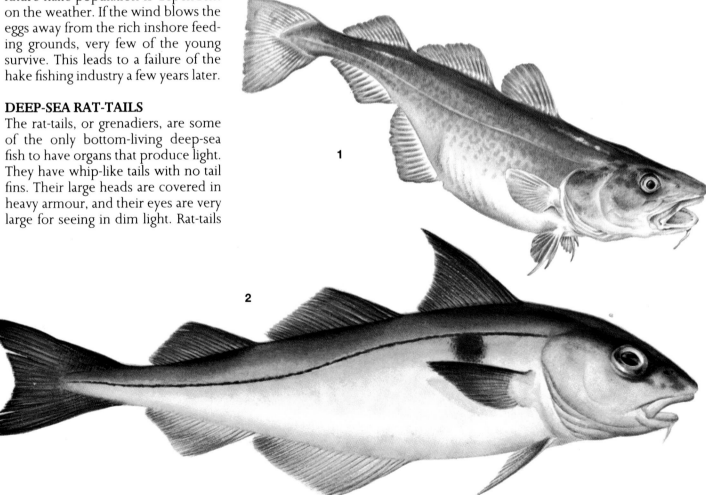

SILVERSIDES, FLYING FISH

As the boat glides through the warm Caribbean water, a group of flying fish leaps out of the water, fins spread wide like wings, tails skimming the surface. The fish skitter across the glittering ocean, then vanish below the surface.

SILVERSIDES, FLYING FISH Orders
Beloniiformes (*160 species*); Atheriniiformes (*240 species*).

■ 🗡

〰 Habitat: sea, fresh water.

▢ Diet: fish, invertebrates.

Distribution: almost worldwide.

Breeding: both external and internal fertilization; some give birth to live young.

Size: length up to 1.5m.

Colour: mostly silvery.

Species mentioned in text:
Grunion (*Leuresthes tenuis*)
Houndfish (*Tylosaurus crocodilus*)

Silversides   Flying fish

Flying fish are very common in the warmer oceans of the world. They are silvery fish with soft spineless fins; the dorsal and anal fins are set far back on the body. The "wings" are formed by the large pectoral fins. Unlike birds, flying fish use their tails, rather than their wings, to fly. They swim rapidly towards the surface with their paired fins folded against their body, then leap out of the water or skim across the surface using the vibrating tail for power. The pectoral fins are used for gliding, not flapping. Flying helps the fish escape from predators like tunas.

Their smaller relatives, the sauries, travel in large shoals, and are sometimes called skippers because of their habit of skipping along the surface.

DANGER – FLYING ARROWS
Needlefish, close relatives of flying fish, are long thin fish with long jaws like forceps. The jaws are armed with

▼Flying fish can reach speeds of 65kph. A succession of short flights can carry them up to 400m in half a minute.

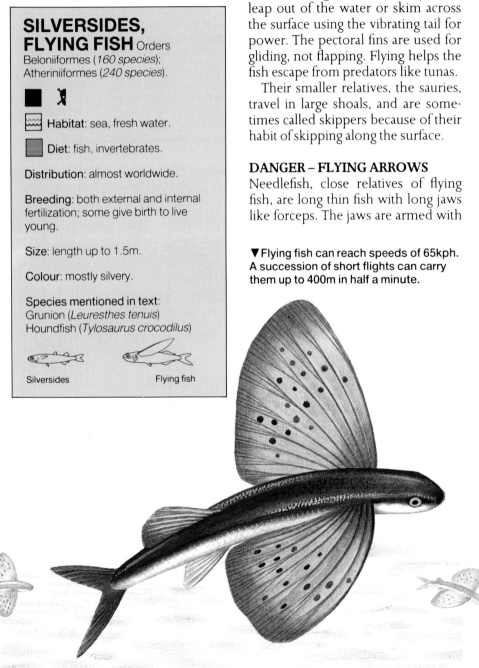

needle-like teeth. When disturbed, the fish leap out of the water and hurtle through the air like arrows. At night they are often attracted to the lights of fishing boats, and can cause serious injuries if they hit fishermen on the head or neck. Some species, such as the houndfish of the North Atlantic, reach lengths of 1.5m and can be very dangerous.

SCOOPING UP FOOD
Halfbeaks are flying fish with extra long lower jaws. They all feed at the surface, using the lower jaw to scoop up insects and other small creatures. The upper jaw clamps shut to hold the prey. Male halfbeaks are famous for their fighting displays, circling each other with their gill covers puffed out and their mouths open.

SKIPPING SILVERSIDES
Silversides are slim silvery fish that often skip along the surface. They are sometimes called shiners because of the silvery bands along their sides. Some live in the ocean, and others in fresh water. An Australian species of rainbow fish has iridescent colours, appearing red, blue or green according to the angle of the light.

A LUNAR CLOCK
Flying fish eggs have long filaments which anchor them well to seaweeds. Their relatives, the halfbeaks, lay their eggs in the open ocean, although a few species retain the eggs inside them until they hatch, giving birth to 20 or more young.

The grunion, a silverside, times its spawning to coincide with the highest tides of the Moon's cycle. It lives off the Pacific coast of North America and comes inshore in spring after the new and full Moon high tides. Scientists believe it detects the phases of the Moon. The fish spawns on beaches only on crests of the highest waves, so the eggs are not covered in water again until 2 weeks later.

▲ ◀Grunion spawn on the beach during the highest tides. The females, swollen with eggs, wriggle their bodies to make depressions in the wet sand. Then they lay their eggs, which the males immediately fertilize. By the time the next wave breaks, the fish are back in the water. The eggs stay hidden safely in the wet sand (left) until the next very high tide. The water stimulates them to hatch, and the young fry are washed far out to sea.

▶Millions of silver grunion gather on the same beaches to spawn, a tempting target for human predators, who simply scoop them up in buckets.

KILLIFISH, LIVE-BEARERS

There is great activity in the aquarium. A rather drab female guppy is being pursued by three males, resplendent in trailing blue or red fins. Impatiently they nudge and butt her, trying to persuade her to mate. The female continues to pursue the small pieces of food drifting through the water, as if uninterested.

Killifish are small, often very brightly coloured fish, popular as aquarium fish. They often have distinctive patterns. The dorsal fin is directly above the anal fin, and the tail fin is blunt and only slightly forked. Their heads are rather flat, and the mouth is directed upwards, as the fish often feed at the water surface.

The live-bearer fish all have internal fertilization. The eggs stay inside the female until they hatch, so she gives birth to up to 200 tiny fish.

FAST-BREEDING GUPPIES
The guppy, about 12cm long, comes from South America and the West Indies. Like other live-bearers, it has internal fertilization. The male guppy's anal fins form a tube to pass sperm into the female's body.

The males are much more attractive than the females, with brilliantly coloured fins, blotches and patterns of orange, blue, green and white. More exotic colours have now been bred by aquarium owners. They become even more brightly coloured during the breeding season, and they pursue the females relentlessly. If a female pauses even for a moment, a male will try to mate with her.

The sperm from a single mating is stored in the female's body, and can fertilize up to 11 broods without any further contact with the male. Guppy eggs have a rich supply of yolk, and develop inside the female until they are born as miniature fish. Guppies

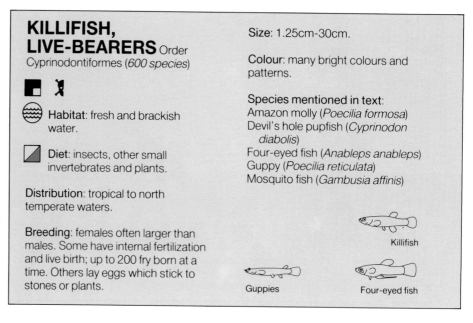

KILLIFISH, LIVE-BEARERS Order
Cyprinodontiformes (*600 species*)

Habitat: fresh and brackish water.

Diet: insects, other small invertebrates and plants.

Distribution: tropical to north temperate waters.

Breeding: females often larger than males. Some have internal fertilization and live birth; up to 200 fry born at a time. Others lay eggs which stick to stones or plants.

Size: 1.25cm-30cm.

Colour: many bright colours and patterns.

Species mentioned in text:
Amazon molly (*Poecilia formosa*)
Devil's hole pupfish (*Cyprinodon diabolis*)
Four-eyed fish (*Anableps anableps*)
Guppy (*Poecilia reticulata*)
Mosquito fish (*Gambusia affinis*)

Killifish

Guppies

Four-eyed fish

can multiply rapidly, since the females are able to produce up to 100 young every 4 weeks given ideal conditions.

In the wild, the tiny newborn fish would all rapidly disappear into the waterweeds. In an aquarium, though, they must be removed quickly, or the adult guppies may mistake them for food and eat them.

INDEPENDENT AMAZONS
The Amazon molly, which lives off the coasts of Texas and Mexico, can reproduce without a male of the same species. Only female Amazons are known. The Amazon mollies mate with males of two related species, but their sperm functions only to stimulate the eggs to develop. It does not contribute to the inheritance of the next generation of Amazon mollies who, like their mother, are all female.

FISH IN THE DESERT
Imagine a dried-up desert pool, just a flat, hard patch of cracked mud. Then a passing thunderstorm fills it with water, and within a few days the pool is teeming with fish. Where have they come from? These are killifish. Their eggs were buried in the dried mud, but within 15 to 30 minutes of getting

wet, they hatched. The pool will not last long as the desert sun will soon evaporate the water. However, these little fish can feed, grow, mate, lay their eggs and die in just 6 weeks.

FOUR-EYED FISH
The four-eyed fish lives in shallow muddy streams in Central America and Mexico. It feeds on insects and other small invertebrates near the surface of the water. Its eyes are large and bulging, like those of a frog, on the top of its head. As it feeds, the eyes are half in and half out of the water.

At the water line, each eye is divided into an upper and a lower part, each with its own cornea and retina (light-sensitive layer). The lens is shaped so that it can focus two images, one from above the water and one from below, simultaneously. When the fish is looking out of water, it uses the upper parts of the eyes, which have good long-distance vision mainly for detecting predators. When looking underwater, it uses the two lower parts.

MOSQUITO-KILLERS
Many guppies and their relatives feed on mosquito larvae as well as other small invertebrates and vertebrates.

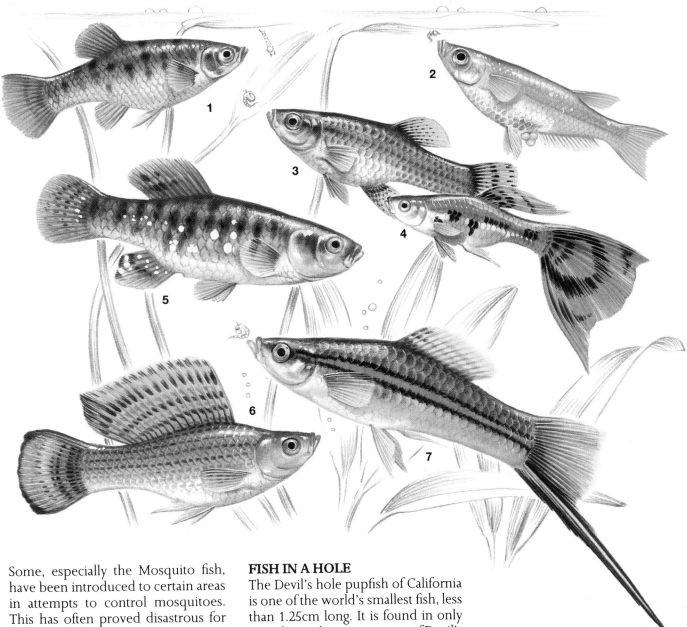

Some, especially the Mosquito fish, have been introduced to certain areas in attempts to control mosquitoes. This has often proved disastrous for local fish populations since, despite their small size, Mosquito fish also feed on the larvae and young of other fish. They have been responsible for the recent extinction of a number of fish species.

The Mosquito fish is an excellent survivor. Unlike the guppy, the female Mosquito fish usually has up to eight broods of young inside her at various stages of development at any one time. She has been known to give birth to hundreds of young at a time.

FISH IN A HOLE

The Devil's hole pupfish of California is one of the world's smallest fish, less than 1.25cm long. It is found in only one place – the warm waters of Devil's Hole, a cave near the edge of Death Valley. The pupfish feed and spawn on a ledge of rock in the water. A few years ago, a local cattle rancher drew so much water from the well that over half the pupfish's rock ledge became exposed. The American government brought a lawsuit against the rancher to stop him pumping any more water out. However, the pupfish remains at serious risk of becoming extinct from other similar drainage schemes.

▲Species of killifish and live-bearer Mosquito fish (1). The ricefish (*Oryzias latipes*) (2), with its eggs, lives in rice paddies in Japan. Female (3) and male (4) guppies. The mummichog (*Fundulus heteroclitus*) (5) is a North American killifish of brackish water that burrows into the mud in winter. The Sailfin molly (*Poecilia latipinna*) (6) is a popular aquarium fish from tropical America. The male Green swordtail (*Xiphophorus helleri*) (7) uses his tail fin in a courtship display to the female.

SCORPIONFISH, GURNARDS

SCORPIONFISH, GURNARDS Order
Scorpaeniformes (*over 1,000 species*)

 Habitat: mostly marine, some fresh water.

Diet: fish, invertebrates.

Distribution: worldwide.

Breeding: seasonal; some species migrate to special spawning grounds. Most lay up to 200,000 eggs on sea bed or rocks; sculpin eggs float to surface; bullheads make nest depression. Other species are live-bearers.

Size: length up to 2m.

Colour: some highly camouflaged in brown, dark red, green, with mottled pattern; others are brilliant orange or pink, or have warning stripes of red and white.

Species mentioned in text:
Bullhead or Miller's thumb (*Cottus gobio*)
Flying gurnard (e.g. *Dactylopterus volitans*)
Lionfish (*Pterois* species)
Oilfish (*Ruvettus pretiosus*)
Sea robins (*Prionotus* and *Trigla* species)
Sculpins (*Cottus* species)
Stone fish (e.g. *Synanceia horrida*)
Zebrafish (*Pterois* species)

Stonefish

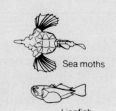
Sea moths

Gurnard

Lionfish

A small fish hovers over the reef, dipping its head to feed on the tiny fronds of seaweed coating the rock. Suddenly, a huge eye in the rock blinks, a gaping chasm opens up, and the fish is sucked inside. The rock was the grotesque head of a scorpionfish, covered in red flaps of seaweed-like skin. The fish was its breakfast.

Scorpionfish and their numerous and varied relatives are all designed for defence, with different combinations of armour-plating, venom and disguise. Scorpionfish and gurnards have a bony ridge reinforcing the cheek just below the eye. Many have bony plates in the skin, especially on the head, and often spines on the gill covers and the dorsal fin. The pectoral fins are large, with wide bases.

MULTI-PURPOSE FINS
The five species of flying gurnard have very large, brightly coloured pectoral fins, used as a display to frighten off predators. The pectoral fins are occasionally spread for gliding above the water surface in brief "flights". The pelvic fins of the true gurnards have another use. They have stiff spines, used like little legs for walking slowly over the seabed or for propping up the fish as it rests on the bottom.

The sea robins use their pectoral fins for both swimming and walking. These fins are in two parts. The upper part has soft rays and is spread and flapped like wings when swimming. By contrast, the lower part has stiff separated rays and is used for walking, and for probing the bottom for food. A sea robin can even turn over rocks with its pectoral fins.

◄Despite its lurid colours, the strange outline of this stone fish is not easily recognizable as that of a fish.

SAFE WITH FATHER

Members of the scorpionfish group reproduce in various ways. Some have internal fertilization and give birth to baby fish. Oilfish females give birth to up to 3,000 young at a time. Most species, though, lay eggs, often in large numbers. These may be laid in rock crevices or on the seabed.

Gurnard eggs float in the plankton, at risk from many dangers, but most sculpin fathers guard their eggs until they hatch. The bullhead, which lives in European streams, makes a kind of nest. The male digs out a hole under a stone, and the female lays the eggs on the roof of this little cave. The stones prevent them being washed away.

◄This lionfish from the Atlantic Ocean has bright colours to warn of the danger from its poison-tipped spines.

▼A deep-water gurnard from Australia (*Lepidotrigla mulhalli*) flashes its pectoral fins in a defensive display. The sudden burst of colour can startle a predator.

DANGEROUS FISH

Zebrafish and lionfish are some of the most spectacular fish of rocky areas and reefs. The rays of the dorsal and pectoral fins are separated and spiny, and the fish often swim with them widely spread. Venom glands at the base of the fin spines deliver poison along a groove in each spine. The fish drift slowly through the water, as if daring other creatures to approach. They will attack other fish that come too close. They sometimes use their large pectoral fins like a net to drive other species into corners of the reef.

MASTERS OF DISGUISE

Several scorpionfish and stone fish are so well camouflaged that it is easy to mistake them for pieces of rock. Their outlines are knobbly; their colours blend well with those of their background – brown or grey, mottled with black and other colours. Tiny flaps of skin resemble the growth of algae on rocks and add to the effect. A few species can even change colour if they move to another background. Some reef-dwelling kinds are brilliantly coloured in pink, orange or red, resembling the brightly coloured sponges and sea squirts that grow over the nearby rocks.

Scorpionfish and stone fish usually stay in much the same area, defending their home ground against other fish. They lie in wait for small fish, crabs and other invertebrates, either leaping out when prey comes within reach, or sucking it in by suddenly opening their huge mouths.

Stone fish are by far the most poisonous fish in the world. They lie in wait to ambush their prey on the seabed or on corals, perfectly camouflaged. Their fin spines inject a poison that can kill a person in 2 hours.

◀This scorpionfish's disguise ideally suits it to a life spent lying in wait for prey. The seaweed-like flaps of skin on its chin and flanks disguise its shape.

STICKLEBACKS, SEA HORSES

A male Three-spined stickleback patrols beside his nest of weeds and sand. A silvery female, swollen with eggs, drifts past above him. Instantly, his eyes have fixed her, and he dances before her, trying to arouse her interest. At last, she turns to follow him down between the weeds to his nest.

STICKLEBACKS, SEA HORSES Order
Gasterosteiformes (*about 250 species*)

◧

≋ Habitat: seas, rivers, lakes.

▨ Diet: small fish, invertebrates.

Distribution: worldwide in tropical and temperate seas; Northern Hemisphere in fresh water.

Breeding: up to 200 eggs; sticklebacks make nests in weeds or on river/sea bed; sea horses and pipefish lay eggs in pouch on belly of male. Parental care common, usually by males.

Size: length up to 1.8m.

Colour: mostly silvery, yellow, black.

Species mentioned in text:
Ten-spined stickleback (*Pungitius pungitius*)
Three-spined stickleback (*Gasterosteus aculeatus*)

Sea horses

Shrimpfish

Sticklebacks

Pipefish

Sticklebacks, sea horses and all their relatives are narrow fish with rather elongated snouts. They lack scales, but their bodies may be covered in bony plates instead. At the front of the dorsal fin are a number of stiff spines, used for defence. If a predator seizes a stickleback in its mouth, the stickleback will erect its dorsal spines and wedge itself in the predator's throat. The predator will soon spit it out, and the stickleback usually swims away unharmed.

FIERCE LITTLE FIGHTERS
Sticklebacks are small fish that live in streams and coastal waters. During the breeding season, the silvery male Three-spined stickleback develops a deep red breast and head and a blue rim to his eyes. He defends an area of stream bed in which he will build his nest and court females.

A female ready to lay her eggs is attracted by the male's red breast, but to a male stickleback, another red fish is a threat and must be driven away. Sticklebacks will fight fiercely to defend their territories. This response is quite instinctive – they will even attack a cardboard sphere that is painted part white, part red.

HOME-BUILDERS
Sticklebacks build nests in which to lay their eggs. The male collects many small pieces of waterweed, and glues them together with sticky material produced by his kidneys. The male Ten-spined stickleback builds a nest among the weeds, while the Three-spined stickleback builds his nest on the sandy stream bed. He anchors it by sucking up mouthfuls of sand and dropping them on the nest.

ON GUARD
The male stickleback guards his eggs until they hatch. The newly hatched sticklebacks still have plenty of yolk in their yolk sacs and live off this for a few days. Their father guards them,

▲A male Three-spined stickleback builds a nest (1) then courts the female with a zig-zag dance. He is attracted by her swollen body. The female enters the nest and, encouraged by the male prodding her belly, lays her eggs there (2). The male immediately swims through the nest and fertilizes them. He fans the eggs to give them plenty of fresh well-aerated water, and removes any snails and caddis larvae from the area around the nest (3).

▲ A ghost pipefish (*Solenostomus paradoxus*) which is found in the warm southern oceans.

◄ A sea horse (*Hippocampus kuda*) from the Indian and Pacific oceans. Sea horses swim in an upright position.

► These shrimpfish (*Aeoliscus strigatus*) often hang head-down. They are so slim that in this position they are not easily recognized as fish.

match their background. Their eyes bulge, and each eye can be moved separately, so that the fish can look in different directions at the same time.

Pipefish are very long and thin. They can glide into crevices where other fish cannot reach. Some live in the sand and gravel of the seabed.

PREGNANT FATHERS

Most male sea horses and pipefish have a brood (egg) pouch on their bellies. During mating, a pair of fish come belly to belly, and the female uses a special tube-like organ called the ovipositor to lay her eggs in the male's pouch. The pouch may hold up to 200 eggs, bulging as if the fish is pregnant. After 4 to 6 weeks the eggs hatch, and the young escape. Often the male has powerful muscle spasms which expel the young, rather like a mammal giving birth. The male may go through this experience as much as three times a year.

chasing away intruders. If a baby fish strays, he will pick it up in his mouth and return it to the nest.

STIFF SWIMMERS

Sea horses and pipefish are protected by rings of hard bony plates which make their bodies very stiff. They have to rely on their transparent dorsal and pectoral fins to propel them through the water. They move up and down by adjusting the amount of air in their swimbladder. All species are able to curl their long tail around weeds or coral to anchor themselves.

Sea horses are well camouflaged, and some can even change colour to

PERCH, BASS

Amid the dark shadows of a sunken wreck lives a huge jewfish. Its silhouette is just visible in the dim light. Only its eyes gleam as they glance from side to side in search of prey. A large lobster lumbers past, unaware of the danger. The jewfish darts forward and, with a snap of its massive jaws, claims the lobster for its supper.

Perch and bass belong to a large group of fish which includes many important food fish. They are thick-bodied fish with well-developed paired fins. The dorsal fin is usually divided into two distinct parts, the front section having very spiny rays. The front rays of the pelvic and anal fins may also be spiny. The tail fin can be quite blunt, as in the bass and groupers, or widely forked, as in the faster-swimming jacks and snappers. Most of these fish are predators, feeding on other fish, crustaceans and other invertebrates.

GIANTS IN HIDING
Groupers, jewfish and sea bass are among the largest of sea fish. The jewfish of the Caribbean and Pacific Ocean can reach a weight of over 300kg. These fish usually live in deep holes, such as caves in coral reefs or on rocky shores. Here they lie in wait

to ambush prey. They do not usually attack divers, but should be treated with respect – the largest of them all, the Queensland grouper of Australia, is up to 4m long, and may weigh as much as 550kg. Some of their freshwater relatives, such as the Nile perch, also reach considerable weights.

GRUNTS, DRUMS, CROAKERS
Certain relatives of perch can make an extraordinary range of sounds underwater. Grunts, drums and croakers are species that can each vibrate strong muscles on either side of the swimbladder, using it just like a drum. The

▶ A grouper leaves its lair to feed on a shoal of small fish.

▼ The Sea goldfish is closely related to the giant groupers. Its busy shoals add to the colourful patchwork and predator-prey relationships of the coral reef.

PERCH, BASS
Order Perciformes (8,000 species)

Habitat: marine and fresh waters.

Diet: mostly invertebrates, fish.

Distribution: worldwide.

Breeding: up to 50,000,000 eggs laid. Some species make nests on sea or river bed. A few are mouth-brooders.

Size: length 2.5cm-3.7m.

Colour: almost every colour occurs.

Species mentioned in text:
Bigeye (*Priacanthus arenatus*)
European perch (*Perca fluviatilis*)
Groupers/sea bass (*Epinephelus* species)
Jewfish (*Epinephelus* species)
Nile perch (*Lates niloticus*)
Queensland grouper (*Ephinephelus lanceolata*)
Pilotfish (e.g. *Naucrates ductor*)
Sea goldfish (*Anthias squamipinnis*)
Striped bass (*Morone saxatilis*)

Perch

Bass, sunfish   Jacks

1

2

3

4

7

8

9

10

74

noise can be heard even out of the water. A wide range of sounds is produced, from quacks and grunts to snores and drumming. The noise is especially loud in the breeding season, when huge groups of fish gather together, drumming furiously. The drumming has been known to confuse submarine pilots, who mistake it for the sound of enemy ships.

THE SAND-MAKERS
Parrotfish feed on coral. Their teeth are fused together to form a beak for biting off lumps of living coral. They also have large grinding teeth in their throat which they use to chew the coral to get at the coral animals inside. The fish cannot digest the limestone skeletons, so these are excreted, producing a fine coral sand that helps to bind the reef together.

Parrotfish feed by day, and hide in a rock crevice to sleep at night. Some species form a slimy mucus cocoon around themselves at night. This may protect them against nocturnal predators. Male and female parrotfish are often different colours, and the young may be yet another colour.

BARBELS AND BIGEYES
Mullets and goatfish feed on the seabed, and have fleshy barbels on their chins to help them find their food. Mullets suck up mud and water, then sieve organic material from the water with filters on their gills. Goatfish feed on worms, crustaceans and molluscs.

The beautiful red bigeye lives in deep water in the warmer parts of the world. Although only 30cm long, this species has eyes more than 2.5cm in diameter to help it see in the dim deep water. This is like a 1.8m-tall person having eyes 15cm across.

FISH AT THE FRONT?
Pilotfish are small bluish fish with dark stripes most of which keep company with sharks. They were once thought to lead sharks to their prey, but the truth is that they have to keep their wits about them to avoid being eaten by the sharks. Each pilotfish is really following the shark in order to feed on scraps left over from its meals, or to pick off external parasites.

SHARKSUCKERS
Sharksuckers, or remoras, all actually travel on sharks and other large fish. Their first dorsal fin forms a sucker with which they cling to the shark's body. As the shark feeds, each sharksucker detaches itself and darts out to steal scraps of food. The whalesucker, which lives on whales, has a sucker that occupies a third of its body.

In parts of the Caribbean, people use sharksuckers to catch turtles. They tie a line to the tail of a sharksucker and release the fish in the water. The sharksucker clings to the turtle, and fish and turtle are pulled in together.

LOTS AND LOTS OF EGGS
Perch and their relatives lay large numbers of eggs. A full-grown female Striped bass may lay 5,000,000 eggs at a time. The eggs all float to the water surface. The European perch scatters up to 300,000 eggs in long ribbons of jelly on plants, rocks and other surfaces. Female darters, small silvery fish that live in streams, burrow into the gravel to lay their eggs. The gravel prevents the eggs being washed away. In other species, the male makes a nest for the eggs, and may guard the eggs and young. Cardinal fish go one better, and carry their eggs in their mouths until they hatch.

CHANGING SEX
Some sea bass, groupers and parrotfish start life as females, then as they grow older, become males. Sea perch can act as either male or female or as both at the same time. Whichever fish of a pair is the most aggressive will act as a female. The other fish will then develop dark bands on its body and act like a male.

◄▲Species of perch, bass and their relatives The Climbing perch (*Anabas testudineus*) (1) uses its fins as legs to crawl from one flooded rice paddy to another. The Crevalle jack (*Caranx hillos*) (2) and Yellowtail snapper (*Ocyurus chrysurus*) (3) travel in shoals. Blue-striped grunt (*Haemulon sciurus*) (4). The Green sunfish (*Lepomis cyanellus*) (5) and Largemouth bass (*Micropterus salmoides*) (6) live in streams and lakes. Bigeye (7). Yellow perch (*Perca flavescens*) (8). The Princess parrotfish (*Scarus taeniopterus*) (9) has a hard beak for eating coral (10).

CICHLIDS, GOURAMIS

Two male Siamese fighting fish are exploring their new aquarium. Their long fins trail gracefully through the water as they weave among the weeds. Suddenly, they come face to face. There is a furious confrontation. Whirling and twisting, they strike out at each other, biting out large chunks of fins and flesh.

▼An archerfish shoots down an insect by spitting droplets of water at it.

Cichlids and gouramis are small to medium-sized freshwater fish, many of which are popular aquarium fish. They have a wide variety of diets, but are mostly meat-eaters. The plant-eaters often have chisel-like teeth in the front of the mouth for cutting weeds or scraping algae off rocks. A few have comb-like teeth for filtering plankton from the water.

Fish-eating types have many sharp pointed teeth for gripping their slippery prey, while the mollusc-eaters all have strong blunt throat teeth used for grinding up the mollusc shells.

A few cichlids are specialists. Some feed on the eggs and young of other mouth-brooding cichlids. They force the parents to literally cough up their offspring. Another group of cichlids feed only on fish scales.

GRACEFUL ANGELS
Cichlids and gouramis have a single dorsal fin, which in some species can be large and beautiful. The pelvic fins are often thin and trailing.

The South American angelfish has a very flat body, and both dorsal and anal fins are very large, so that its body is almost circular. The tips of all the fins trail off into thin filaments. As the fish swims slowly among the weeds, it has a dreamy appearance. This has made it popular in aquaria. Angelfish grow up to 30cm long in the wild.

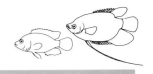

AIMING FOR INSECTS

Archerfish live in the river estuaries and mangrove swamps of South-east Asia. They all have flattened bodies, large eyes and an upward-directed mouth that looks as if it is pouting. They catch insects by spitting a stream of water droplets at them and knocking them into the water. The drops are formed in a tube made by pressing a fleshy part of the tongue against a groove in the roof of the mouth. If the insect is near the water, an archerfish may leap out of the water and seize the insect in its jaws instead.

FIGHTING FISH

Male cichlids and gouramis become markedly aggressive in the breeding season. The males set up territories in which to court the females and bring up their families. They defend these areas against other males. First, they will try a threat display: both fish raise their dorsal fins, and move slowly towards each other, lashing their tails to slap water against their rival. If this does not work, the fighting starts, and they start mouth-pulling. Eventually, one of the fish, usually the smaller one, tires and swims away.

BLOWING BUBBLES

Numerous gouramis and fighting fish make bubble nests at the surface of the water. The male blows bubbles through a sticky mucus. The female sheds her heavy eggs into the water, and the male has to get them up to the nest. A male fighting fish will turn the female upside down as he sheds his sperm. The eggs are fertilized as soon as they are produced, and the male catches them in his mouth and sticks them to the bubble nest.

A MOUTHFUL OF BABIES

Most cichlids take good care of their eggs and young. Both mother and father keep an eye on the fry: if they stray too far, their parents pick them up in their mouths and move them to a safe place. Some cichlids guard their eggs in their mouths, too.

Tilapias, African cichlids that are often reared as food fish, start by making a nest for the eggs. The male makes the nest and guards it against other males. He displays to attract females to lay their eggs in it, usually about 20 at a time. As soon as he has shed his sperm over them, the female takes both eggs and sperm into her mouth. The eggs are fertilized here and remain safe until they hatch, as their mother, unable to feed, hides in a sheltered place.

After the eggs hatch, the young fish swarm around their mother, apparently attracted by the dark colour of her mouth and eyes. Later they will follow her around in a tight shoal.

STICKING TO MUM AND DAD

The discus fish of the Amazon basin in South America also keep their eggs in their mouths. After hatching the fry become attached to plants and rocks by tiny threads while they use up the yolk in their yolk sacs. When they are old enough to swim around, they make for their parents' bodies. There, for several days, they feed on a special mucus secreted by the adults' skin.

▲ Two male gouramis press their lips together, but not for love. They are threatening each other, each trying to push the other away.

▼ A female mouth-brooder cichlid keeps her eggs safely in her mouth until they hatch. The newly hatched fry return to their mother's mouth if danger threatens.

BUTTERFLYFISH, DAMSELFISH

A group of Red-striped butterflyfish are cruising among the branches of coral, their brilliant yellow bodies glowing through the dim blue water. From time to time they pause to nibble at the coral, or glide into crevices in search of small reef creatures. Their black and white faces appear and disappear as they twist and turn, like the opening and closing of a butterfly's wings.

BUTTERFLYFISH, DAMSELFISH Order

Perciformes (*about 8,000 species*)

Habitat: mostly shallow seas and reefs.

Diet: various invertebrates.

Distribution: tropical and subtropical regions worldwide.

Breeding: produce many tiny eggs. Some species have parental care.

Size: length 6-60cm.

Colour: brilliantly coloured, often with patterns of stripes and blocks of colour. Females and juveniles may differ in colour.

Species mentioned in text:
Copperband butterflyfish (*Chelmon rostratus*)
Forceps butterflyfish (*Forcipiger longirostris*)
Red-striped butterflyfish (*Chaetodon lunula*)
Rock beauty (*Holocanthus tricolor*)

Butterflyfish

Damselfish

Clownfish

Butterflyfish and the closely related angelfish are small- to medium-sized fish very common on coral reefs. They have tall, flat bodies, and are almost invisible when viewed head-on. This shape enables them to slip very easily between the branches of coral and cracks and crevices on the reef. They have long dorsal fins, with the spiny portion often erected so that each ray can be clearly seen.

TRAILING FILAMENTS

Butterflyfish feed on small invertebrates, including coral polyps. The head tapers rapidly to a narrow snout with a small mouth equipped with bristle-like teeth. Some species, such as the Copperband butterflyfish and the Forceps butterflyfish, specialize in feeding in crevices, and have very long, narrow snouts.

Angelfish look much like butterflyfish, but their dorsal and anal fins are drawn out into long trailing filaments. There is a long spine at the base of the gill cover. The lips are often a different colour from the rest of the body, as if they were wearing lipstick. Whereas young butterflyfish resemble their parents, young angelfish often have quite different colours and patterns.

DISGUISES AND CONFUSION

Although most of these fish are brightly coloured, they are often disguised. Among the brightly coloured corals and sponges, butterflyfish are not so conspicuous as you might imagine, and their brilliant patterns can actually be good camouflage.

Many predators can recognize their prey by its shape – in this case, a fish shape. Some butterflyfish have blocks of colour with bold shapes that are not at all fish-shaped. The Rock beauty has a yellow head and belly, black sides and a yellow tail. From a distance it looks as if the head is separate from the tail. The fish shape has disappeared. Stripes can also help to break up a fish's outline.

LOOK – NO EYES!

Another giveaway feature is the fish's eyes. Even plainly coloured butterflyfish and angelfish often have a dark stripe running down the face through each eye, to disguise its shape. Some species go a step further and have false eyespots near their tails. If a predator takes a nip out of the tail, the fish will probably survive, whereas if it is attacked around the eye, it is likely to die. The fish reinforces this disguise by swimming slowly backwards, so that it appears to be swimming in the direction in which the false eyes are pointing. When disturbed it shoots rapidly forward, to the confusion of the predator.

LIVING WITH DANGER

Damselfish resemble slightly plump butterflyfish. Despite their small size, they fiercely defend a small patch of reef or rock where they hunt for food, even threatening predators larger than themselves. Clownfish live among the stinging tentacles of sea anemones, even laying their eggs there. Other fish would be injured by the stinging cells, but the clownfish appear to be unharmed. They feed on the left-overs from the anemone's meals and gain protection because their enemies do not dare to approach the anemone.

▶ **Some species of butterflyfish and their relatives** Red-tail surgeonfish (*Acanthurus achilles*) (1). The Saddleback butterflyfish (*Chaetodon ephippium*) (2) disguises its shape. Clownfish (*Amphiprion percula*) (3) in a sea anemone, probably protected from the stinging tentacles by a slimy mucus coat. Regal angelfish (*Pygoplites diacanthus*) (4). Copperband butterflyfish (5) has a long snout for probing in crevices. The Moorish idol (*Zanclus canescens*) (6). South American leaffish (*Monocirrhus polyacanthus*) (7) which floats in the water like a dead leaf, waiting for unsuspecting fish to come close enough for it to seize them.

MACKEREL, TUNA

A shoal of mackerel moves effortlessly through the Pacific Ocean, the fish's bodies undulating gently from side to side. Sunlight picks out the rippling stripes on their backs, making it difficult to distinguish one fish from another. Behind the shoal, a large Blue marlin is approaching fast. When the marlin reaches the mackerel, it leaps in among them, slashing with its spear-shaped beak.

MACKEREL, TUNA
Order Perciformes (*about 8,000 species*)

⬛

≋ Habitat: open sea.

⬛ Diet: fish, invertebrates.

Distribution: worldwide.

Breeding: produce up to 5 million small eggs, which float to surface.

Size: length 25cm-5m.

Colour: most green or blue on back, with white belly and dark stripes.

Species mentioned in text:
Blue marlin (*Makaira nigricans*)
Horse mackerel (*Trachurus trachurus*)
Portuguese man-o'-war fish (*Nomeus gronovii*)
Sailfish (*Istiophorus platypterus*)
Swordfish (*Xiphias gladius*)

Mackerel

Swordfish

Mackerel and tuna all have elegant torpedo shapes, with deeply forked tails. They have separate spiny and soft dorsal fins, but their special characteristic is the rows of small finlets between the second dorsal fin and the tail and the anal fins and the tail. One or more narrow ridges run back towards the body from the tail. They are popular food fish, since they often travel close to the coast and entire shoals can be caught at a time.

HIGH-SPEED HUNTERS
Tuna are fast swimmers, cruising at up to 48kph. They rely on their powerful tails for propulsion. Unlike most fish, tuna can maintain their body temperature up to 10°C higher than the surrounding water. This helps to keep their muscles working fast even when travelling in cool water. Tuna can outswim many predators, although not their main enemy, the Killer whale.

Mackerel and tuna travel in large shoals, feeding on other fish and on invertebrates. Some species migrate to special feeding or spawning sites at certain times of year. All of them have large mouths that extend almost to their eyes. Because they swim fast, water flows over their gills as they go and no pumping effort is necessary. They have a very large gill area which enables them to take in sufficient oxygen to swim rapidly.

SURROUNDED BY STINGS
Several mackerel and their relatives seek a strange protection from their enemies: they live deep among the tentacles of jellyfish. The Portuguese man-o'-war fish lives under its namesake, feeding on scraps abandoned by the jellyfish. Young Horse mackerel live under the Sombrero jellyfish. Predators will not approach the jellyfish for fear of their stinging tentacles, but exactly how the mackerel survive unscathed is not known.

AEROBATIC FISH
Marlins are famous for their aerobatics when caught on a fishing line. They will leap many times into the air, and sometimes succeed in throwing off the hook. Since they can weigh over 700kg, this presents quite a challenge to the fisherman. Sailfish are also large fish, up to 2.5m long, and popular with sportsmen. The large bright blue

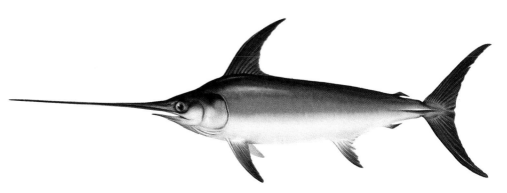

▲ The swordfish has a flat, narrow snout edged with many small sharp teeth like the blade of a saw. This "sword" is probably used to slash at prey. Swordfish are famous for ramming wooden fishing boats, and can even pierce a hole through copper sheeting. One boat reported a swordfish hole 56cm deep.

dorsal fin can lie flat against the body in a special groove when the fish is swimming at speed.

Sailfish and marlins use their spear-like upper jaws to impale their prey. They speed through schools of fish, stunning them with their snout, then returning to pick up the dead and injured fish. Unlike their relatives, the mackerel and tunas, swordfish, sailfish and marlin hunt alone or in pairs. There would be a risk of hurting each other if they got too close during a hunt. Baby sailfish and marlins have jaws of equal length until they are large enough to start killing fish.

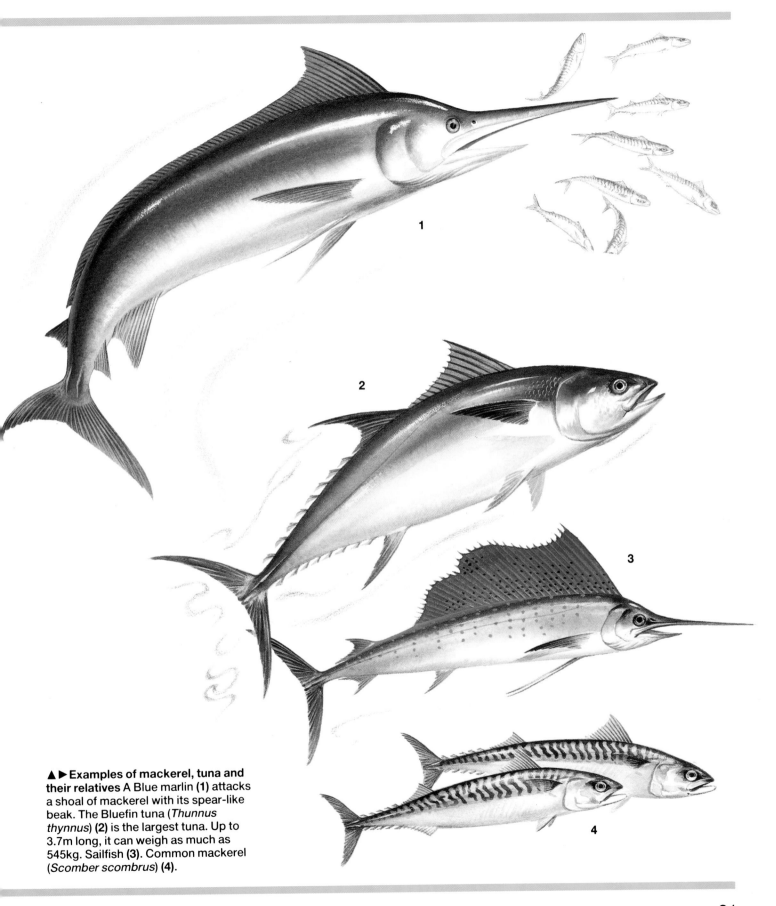

▲▶Examples of mackerel, tuna and
their relatives A Blue marlin (1) attacks
a shoal of mackerel with its spear-like
beak. The Bluefin tuna (*Thunnus
thynnus*) (2) is the largest tuna. Up to
3.7m long, it can weigh as much as
545kg. Sailfish (3). Common mackerel
(*Scomber scombrus*) (4).

BARRACUDAS, WRASSES

In a quiet corner of the coral reef, a group of large blue and yellow striped fish, Painted sweetlips, wait patiently, watching the antics of a small blue and black striped fish. The cleanerfish appears to be dancing in front of them. A sweetlips moves forward, presenting itself broadside on to the cleanerfish and raising its gill covers. The little fish darts forward, noses its way under a gill cover and starts to feed, picking off several tiny parasites.

BARRACUDAS, WRASSES Order Perciformes
(*about 8,000 species*).

- Habitat: seas and coral reefs.

- Diet: fish and invertebrates.

Distribution: warm and temperate regions.

Breeding: produce several thousand eggs. Barracuda eggs float. Wrasse eggs may float, or are laid in nests and guarded by one or both parents.

Size: length 6cm-3m.

Colour: barracudas blue-grey; wrasses in many colours, most often green, marked with red, yellow, blue.

Species mentioned in text:
Bluehead (*Thalassoma bifasciatum*)
Cleanerfish (e.g. *Labroides dimidiatus*)
Yellowtail wrasse (*Coris gaimardi*)

Barracudas   Wrasses

Wrasses are colourful bottom-feeding fish of shallow coastal water and coral reefs. They feed on a wide variety of invertebrates, including hard-shelled crustaceans and molluscs. They have large pouting mouths with thick lips that can stretch forward to seize a tasty morsel. Their front teeth protrude like forceps to pick up small animals or nip out chunks of fins or flesh from other fish. Their jaws contain strong teeth for crushing and chewing shells. Many species burrow in the sand and sleep at night, but can readily be seen by day, busily hunting for food.

AN INFINITE VARIETY
Wrasses show an enormous range of colours. Many species change colour as they grow older, and adopt yet another colour during their breeding season. The Yellowtail wrasse has a bright red body with large white blotches edged in black and a yellow tail. Males of the bluehead are green with a blue head and black collar, while the females are yellow all over with black blotches.

WHERE FISH STAND IN LINE
Many small wrasses feed on the skin parasites of larger fish and also remove their damaged scales. Each cleaner-fish sets up shop in a special territory, and larger fish visit it to be cleaned. Fish that would normally prey on others the size of the cleaner wrasses, or on each other, queue patiently for service, with no sign of aggression. It is as if a special truce exists in the cleaner's territory.

Many wrasses make nests of sand or algae in which to lay their eggs. The nest is usually hidden in a crevice, and the male may invite several females to lay their eggs in it. The eggs and young are guarded by one or both parents.

FEARSOME PREDATORS
Barracudas look like typical predatory fish. They are all long and cylindrical, well streamlined, and with a narrow head. Their long lower jaws stick out beyond the upper jaws to display a fearsome array of needle-sharp teeth. Up to 2m long, they are feared by swimmers, but appear to follow them more from curiosity than from any ill intent. Barracudas seem to be particularly attracted to shiny objects like underwater cameras. When they are small, they travel in groups (schools), but the adults hunt alone.

▶ This little fish appears to be doomed, but in fact it is quite safe. It is a cleaner wrasse, and it is removing parasites from the mouth of a Monstrous sweetlips (*Plectorhynchus* species). The larger fish has deliberately opened its mouth for the cleaner to enter.

▼ A barracuda caught in a shaft of light off the coast of Florida.

BLENNIES, GOBIES

On the wet mud between the mangrove roots, two mudskippers are arguing over a patch of mud. The present owner is sitting on a ridge surrounding the entrance to his burrow, propped up on his fins. Facing him is the challenger. The two fish bob heads furiously, flicking their dorsal fins up and down and making mock advances towards each other. Suddenly the defender darts across the mud towards the intruder, who turns and shuffles away.

Blennies and gobies are small fish with large frog-like bulging eyes and a habit of resting propped up on their stiff pelvic fins. In blennies the two dorsal fins are usually joined together and run the whole length of the body. The anal fin is also especially long and narrow. In gobies, the two dorsal fins are distinct, and the first few rays of the spiny dorsal fin are often long and prominent.

Most species of these fish live on the seabed, and are well-camouflaged and difficult to see until they move. They feed on worms, small crustaceans and other types of invertebrate, which they find mainly by sight.

COMING UP FOR AIR

Many species of blenny and goby are quite mobile on land, flicking themselves along with either their pelvic or pectoral fins. Some blennies can leap from one rock pool to another at low tide. They can trap air and water in their gill chambers and survive for several hours out of water.

The mudskippers of the African mangrove swamps can also take in oxygen through the moist lining of the mouth and throat. The fish often appear to be panting, when they are really just opening their mouths to take in fresh air.

Mudskippers hop along the mud on their pelvic fins, which are thick and fleshy and look like little legs. They can even climb the mangrove roots to escape from predators if they cannot get back to their burrows in time. As in many gobies, the bases of their pelvic fins are joined to form a sucking disc that helps them grip on vertical surfaces.

A MEAN DECEPTION

The Sabre-toothed blenny is a pretty little fish, boldly striped in blue and black, but it has some unattractive habits. It closely resembles a cleaner-fish, a fish that picks off the parasites from the skin and gills of larger fish. Larger fish recognize the "cleaner" by its bright colours, and wait patiently to be cleaned. The Sabre-toothed blenny nips in and bites a chunk out of the skin or fins of the unsuspecting fish.

UNUSUAL NURSERIES

Males of many species of blenny and goby defend a nest or other nursery against intruders, displaying to attract females to lay their eggs there. Once the eggs are laid, one of the parents will guard them until they hatch.

Mudskippers build nests up to 1.5m across in the mud. The Sand goby tips up an empty mollusc shell so that the opening is on the seabed, then digs a tunnel into it. The Marbled blenny

BLENNIES, GOBIES
Order Perciformes (*about 8,000 species*)

 Habitat: mostly marine, near sea bed, a few freshwater species.

Diet: worms, crustaceans, molluscs.

Distribution: worldwide, mostly tropical and subtropical.

Breeding: eggs usually laid in nests or other shelters, and guarded by male or female parent.

Size: 1.3cm-1.5m.

Colour: most well camouflaged in browns, greys and greens.

Species mentioned in text:
Dwarf pygmy goby (*Pandaka pygmaea*)
Marbled blenny (*Paraclinus marmoratus*)
Mudskippers (*Periophthalmus* and *Beleophthalmus* species)
Sabre-toothed blenny (*Aspinodontis taeniatus*)
Sand goby (*Pomatoschistus minutus*)

Blennies   Gobies

lays its eggs inside a sponge and stays to guard them. The water currents circulating through the sponge bring the eggs a good supply of oxygen.

The hatchlings (fry) resemble their parents and grow fast. However, the adults of the Dwarf pygmy goby of the Philippines are not only the smallest fish in the world, they are the smallest vertebrates on Earth. Each measures only 1.3cm long when fully grown.

▶A blenny keeps an eye out for danger on a coral reef in the Middle East.

▼Mudskippers have eyes so well adapted for seeing in air that they can even catch insects in flight.

FLATFISH

The sand stirs beneath the diver's feet as a large flounder shakes off its concealing layer of sand and takes to the open water. The fish's whole body seems to undulate up and down as it swims. After a short distance, it sinks to the seabed again. There it ducks its head into the sand a few times to flip sand over its back, and becomes almost invisible again. Only its bulging eyes and the tip of its mouth can be seen above the sand, on the look-out for prey and danger.

At first glance a flatfish looks as if it has a wide body with two long fins forming fringes at the sides. In fact, it is tall and thin, but it spends most of its life lying on its side. It swims by flexing its body from side to side, although it appears to be bending up and down because it moves on its side too. Flatfish include such familiar edible fish as flounders, plaice, halibut and turbot. The smaller species feed on worms, molluscs and crustaceans; the larger species hunt other fish.

▶ The twisted face of this adult flatfish is a reminder of the changes the animal has gone through while growing up.

▼ A newly hatched flatfish resembles any other kind of fish, with an eye on each side and a horizontal mouth. As the larva grows, one eye travels to the other side of the head, the mouth twists, and the fish starts to lie on one side.

FLATFISH Order Pleuronectiformes (*about 500 species*)

Habitat: sea and fresh water.

Diet: crustaceans, molluscs and other invertebrates; fish.

Distribution: worldwide.

Breeding: lay large numbers of small eggs which float to the surface. Larvae undergo dramatic change in shape and in position of body organs.

Size: length up to 2.75m.

Colour: dull grey, brown or black, often mottled, rarely striped, with pale belly. Most can change colour.

Species mentioned in text:
Flounder (e.g. *Platichthys flesus*)
Halibut (*Hippoglossus* species)
Plaice (*Pleuronectes* species)
Turbot (*Scophthalmus maxima*)

Flatfish

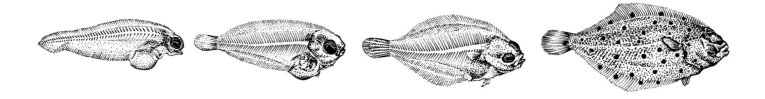

FLAT-FACED HUNTERS

Flatfish catch their prey in various ways. Some flounders and halibut are active by day, relying on their sight to find their victims. They will chase fish through the water. Other species, for example the soles, hunt at night, and find their prey, mostly molluscs and worms, by smell. Plaice use both sight and smell to find their food, often lying well-concealed on the seabed until crabs or other prey pass nearby.

Most flatfish suck in their victims by suddenly opening their mouths. Larger species may swallow entire fish. Halibut pursue prey through the open water, and have been known to catch seabirds, probably seizing them while swimming. Female halibut can grow to 2.75m long, and weigh 320kg.

LIFE ON THE BOTTOM

Flatfish are very well camouflaged. Their upper side is brown or grey, often mottled, and they can change colour to match their background. Some flatfish can even manage a fair match if placed on a chequerboard. The underside is white. The dorsal and anal fins form a fringe that conceals the fish's shadow when it is lying on the seabed. This camouflage hides them not only from their enemies but also from their prey. Many flatfish add to their camouflage by flicking sand over themselves.

RIGHT-EYED OR LEFT-EYED?

Each flatfish species usually has its eyes on one particular side of the face. Left-eye flounders always have both

▲Adult flatfish can change their colour and pattern to match their background, as this flounder demonstrates.

eyes on the left side of the body, which becomes their top side. The right-eyed flounders, which include the plaice and halibut, have their eyes on the right side, but left-eyed individuals are occasionally found.

LIFE AT THE TOP

Flatfish start their lives at the surface of the water. The females lay many eggs that contain oil droplets which help them to float. Female turbot lay up to 9,000,000 eggs at a time. The eggs hatch in a few days, and the larvae feed among the plankton for a few weeks before sinking to the bottom.

TRUNKFISH, PUFFERFISH

Keeping its head down, a filefish sways gently in the water currents, copying the movements of the seaweed among which it is feeding. The rows of colourful blotches on its body disguise its outline, and in this upright position it is hardly recognizable as a fish. The danger passes, and the filefish returns to probing between the weeds with its slender snout for small worms.

Trunkfish and pufferfish are very stiff angular fish covered in an armour of bony plates. This stops them flexing their bodies to swim. They have virtually no pelvic fins, and rely on their pectoral fins for propulsion. They use the tail fin for steering. The first dorsal fin is very small or absent. The second, soft, dorsal fin is near the back of the body, directly in line with the quite prominent anal fins.

Most of these fish live near coasts in tropical seas, where they feed on small invertebrates. Their mouths are small, their snouts taper, and their jaws form a beak for dealing with hard shellfish.

HIGH-PRESSURE FEEDERS

Trunkfish, boxfish and triggerfish feed mainly on worms, crustaceans and molluscs. They will stand on their heads and squirt jets of water at the sand or mud to expose their prey, which they then suck up. To break open the hard shells, not only do they have their hard beaks, they also have strong chisel-shaped crushing teeth.

Triggerfish have large spines on the dorsal fin, which can be raised and locked in place. The front spine is fixed in position by the second spine, which slides forward to hold it. The triggerfish uses this spine to jam itself firmly in crevices, so that its enemies cannot pull it out.

A DANGEROUS DELICACY

Trunkfish and pufferfish are often regarded as a great delicacy in Japan, but it can be very dangerous to eat them. They contain a poison, tetradoxin,

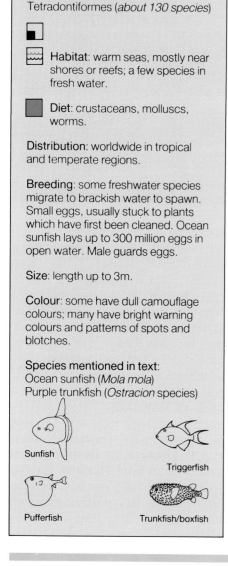

TRUNKFISH, PUFFERFISH Order
Tetradontiformes (*about 130 species*)

■

〜 Habitat: warm seas, mostly near shores or reefs; a few species in fresh water.

▨ Diet: crustaceans, molluscs, worms.

Distribution: worldwide in tropical and temperate regions.

Breeding: some freshwater species migrate to brackish water to spawn. Small eggs, usually stuck to plants which have first been cleaned. Ocean sunfish lays up to 300 million eggs in open water. Male guards eggs.

Size: length up to 3m.

Colour: some have dull camouflage colours; many have bright warning colours and patterns of spots and blotches.

Species mentioned in text:
Ocean sunfish (*Mola mola*)
Purple trunkfish (*Ostracion* species)

Sunfish

Triggerfish

Pufferfish

Trunkfish/boxfish

▼A Purple trunkfish on a reef near Hawaii. Its body is almost triangular in cross section and brilliantly patterned to warn of danger. Like many trunkfish, when disturbed it gives off a poisonous substance that can kill nearby fish.

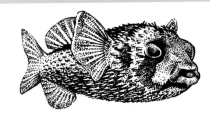

▲ As a porcupinefish puffs up its body, the spines on its scales stick out more, making it almost impossible for a predator to swallow the fish.

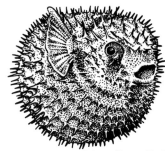

◀ A Pacific cowfish (*Lactoria* species). Cowfish are really boxfish with two horn-like lumps on their heads. They use their pectoral fins to scull themselves along.

which is powerful enough to kill a person. The poison is stored in various parts of the body, which must be removed immediately after the death of the fish to avoid poisoning. Cooks are specially trained to prepare this "fugu", but even so, some people die every year from eating it.

ALL PUFFED UP

Pufferfish and porcupinefish inflate themselves when in danger, or if they are picked up and taken out of the water. This is done by swallowing air or water and storing it in part of the gut. When the fish let the air out again, they make a belching sound. Once inflated, pufferfish can support the weight of a full-grown man. Puffed up porcupinefish are often dried and sold as souvenirs.

A pufferfish will sometimes puff up if it encounters another pufferfish on its territory. This makes it look larger and more threatening, and hopefully will persuade the intruder to go away. It will also swallow air if it is stranded

in a rock pool as the tide goes out. The fish floats belly up at the surface of the water. The air then passes slowly into the blood and reaches the gills, where it provides oxygen to compensate for the lack of water.

FISH WITH NO TAIL

The Ocean sunfish is often called a headfish, because it appears to have a head, but no tail. Its tail is simply a narrow fringe. Its body is almost round, and can reach a great size, up to 3m long and 1,000kg in weight. It holds the record for egg production, laying 300,000,000 eggs at a time.

The sunfish sculls along in the open ocean, using its two vertical fins. It feeds on small soft creatures such as squid and crustaceans, and is one of the few fish known to eat jellyfish. It was given the name sunfish because it is sometimes found lying on its side at the surface, as if sunbathing. The reason for this behaviour is unknown; such specimens may simply be tired, sick or dying fish.

GLOSSARY

Algae Simple plant-like organisms not made up of stems, leaves and roots. Seaweeds are algae as is the green slime or colour film often seen in water.

Anal fin The single fin on a fish's belly nearest the tail.

Antennae Feelers.

Bacteria Microscopic organisms each of which consists of a single cell that lacks a distinct nuclear membrane and has a cell wall of a unique type. Some bacteria are food for other organisms. Others decompose organic material or cause diseases in plants and animals.

Barbels Short fleshy tentacles near the mouths of some fish, used for tasting and touching.

Body temperature The temperature of the interior of an animal's body.

Camouflage Colour and patterns on an animal's skin that allow it to blend with its surroundings.

Carnivore An animal that feeds mainly on the flesh of another animal.

Cartilaginous Made of cartilage. Cartilage is a flexible supporting material made by the body; it is softer than bone.

Caudal fin Tail fin.

Class The division of animal classification above Order.

Cocoon A protective covering.

Cornea The transparent outer covering of the eye.

Courtship The period when an animal tries to attract a mate.

Crustaceans Shelled creatures, like crabs, lobsters, shrimps, prawns, krill and copepods.

Detritus Broken down dead plant and animal material.

Display A typical pattern of behaviour associated with important aspects of an animal's life, such as courtship, mating, nesting and defending territory.

Distribution The area in the world in which a species or group of species is found.

Dorsal fin The fin on a fish's back. Many fish have two dorsal fins.

Ectothermic animals Animals that are unable to produce their own internal heat. Their body temperature depends on how warm (or cool) their surroundings are.

Embryo A young animal developing within its egg.

Endangered species One whose numbers have dropped so low that it is in danger of becoming extinct.

External fertilization Joining of eggs and sperm outside the female's body; in fish it happens in water.

Extinct Died out; refers to a population or species that no longer exists.

Family In classification of animals, a group of species which share many features in common and are thought to be related, such as all the mackerel.

Filament A thin thread-like structure.

Filter-feeders Animals that feed by sieving food from the water through a kind of mesh.

Fin rays The stiff supports in fins, made of bone or cartilage.

Fry Very young fish.

Genus The division of animal classification below Family and above Species. In the fish world there are about 3,860 recognized genera.

Gill A structure in water-living animals through which exchange of oxygen and carbon dioxide takes place.

Gill chamber A body cavity enclosing the gills and into which fresh (oxygenated) water enters and used (deoxygenated) water leaves during respiration.

Gill rakers Stiff comb-like structures on the inside of the arch supporting the gills, which strain particles from the water flowing past them.

Glands Organs that produce a special chemical (secretion) that is passed (secreted) to the outside world.

Habitat The surroundings in which an animal lives, including the plant life, other animals, physical surroundings and climate.

Hatching The moment when a young fish emerges from the egg.

Internal fertilization Joining of eggs and sperm inside a female's body.

Invertebrate Any animal without a backbone, e.g. insects, worms, crabs and mussels.

Juvenile A young animal that is no longer a baby, but is not yet fully adult.

Larva An early stage in the life-cycle of an animal after it hatches from the egg. Usually it has a very different form from the adult, for example an eel leptocephalus larva.

Lateral line A system in fish of sensitive structures that can detect vibrations in the water. These structures often lie in a groove running along each side of the fish and branching over its head.

Light organs Small structures in the bodies of fish and some other animals that produce light.

Live-bearers Fish whose eggs hatch inside the female's body, so that she gives birth to baby fish instead of laying eggs.

Metamorphosis A change in structure of an animal as it goes from one stage of its life history to the next, as when any larva changes to an adult.

Migration The long-distance movement of animals. It is typically seasonal, e.g. between shallow-water breeding grounds in spring and deeper water in summer.

Milt A milky liquid that contains the sperms of the male fish which fertilize the eggs of the female.

Mimic An animal that imitates another animal, usually for protection from predators.

Molluscs Soft-bodied animals, usually with protective shells, including snails, cockles, mussels, limpets, octopuses and squids.

Mouth-brooder A fish that keeps its eggs, and sometimes also its young, safe by holding them in its mouth.

Mucus A sticky, slimy substance produced by some membranes, such as the skin of fish.

Operculum Cover over the gills.

Order The division of animal classification below Class and above Family. There are about 37 recognized orders in the fish world.

Parasite An animal or plant that lives on another animal or plant and feeds on it. The animal or plant on which it lives is called the host.

Pectoral fins The pair of fins on a fish's sides, usually situated just behind the gill cover.

Pelvic fins The pair of fins on a fish's belly in front of the anal fin.

Plankton Tiny microscopic floating plants and animals that live at or near the surface of seas and lakes.

Predator An animal that hunts and kills other animals, its prey.

Prey The animals that are hunted by a predator.

Ray A skeletal structure, usually of bone or cartilage, which supports and gives shape to the fins of fish.

Scales Small bony or horny plates produced in the skin that overlap to protect the fish's body.

School Also called a shoal, a large group of fish that go around together. Some fish shoals contain millions of fish, others contain only a dozen or so individuals.

Shoal *See* School.

Solitary Living alone for most of the time.

Spawning Laying eggs in water. The eggs of fish and frogs are often referred to as spawn.

Species The division of animal classification below Genus; a group of animals of the same structure that can breed together.

Spiracle A round hole through which a fish's gill chamber opens to the outside. Spiracles are found only in certain groups of fish, such as rays and lampreys.

Streamlined Shaped to offer minimum resistance to the air and water. A streamlined body is usually more or less torpedo-shaped, with a smooth outline and no large protrusions.

Sub-tropics The two warm regions bordering the tropics to the north and south of the equator.

Swimbladder A gas-filled bag inside the fish's body which helps it to float. The fish can adjust the amount of gas in the swimbladder in order to rise or sink in the water. Not all fish have swimbladders.

Temperate A climate that is not too hot and not too cold. Temperate zones lie between the sub-tropics and the cold high latitude regions in both hemispheres.

Tentacle A long slender flexible structure, used for feeling, tasting or grasping.

Territory The area in which an animal or group of animals lives and defends against intruders.

Tropics Strictly, the region between latitudes 23° north and south of the equator. Tropical regions are typically very hot and humid.

Vertebrates Animals with backbones. Fish are aquatic vertebrates, amphibians live both on land and in water, while reptiles, birds and mammals are terrestrial vertebrates.

INDEX

Scientific names

The first name of each double-barrel Latin name refers to the *Genus*, the second to the *species*. Single names not in *italic* refer to a class, order, family or sub-family and are cross referenced to the Common name index.

FURTHER READING

Alexander, R. McNeill (ed) (1986), *The Collins Encyclopedia of Animal Biology*, Collins, London.

Banister, K. and Campbell, A. (eds) (1985), *The Encyclopedia of Underwater Life*, Collins, London.

Berra, T.M. (1981), *An Atlas of the Distribution of the Freshwater Fish Families of the World*, University of Nebraska Press, Lincoln, Nebraska, and London.

Berry, R.J. and Hallam, A. (eds) (1986), *The Collins Encyclopedia of Animal Evolution*, Collins, London.

Bond, C.E. (1979), *Biology of Fishes*, Saunders College Publishing, Philadelphia.

Hoar, W. S. and Randall, D. J. (eds) (1969-), *Fish Physiology*, Academic Press, London and New York.

Hoese, H. D. and Moore, H. D. (1977), *Fishes of the Gulf of Mexico, Texas, Louisiana and Adjacent Waters*, Texas A. & M. University Press, College Station, Texas.

Lake, J.S. (1971), *Freshwater Fishes and Rivers of Australia*, Thomas Nelson, Melbourne.

Marshall, N. B. (1971), *Explorations in the Life of Fishes*, Harvard University Press, Cambridge, Massachusetts.

Marshall, N. B. (1965), *The Life of Fishes*, Weidenfeld and Nicholson, London.

Midgalski, E.C. and Fichter, G.S. (1977), *The Fresh and Salt Water Fish of the World*, Octopus Books, London.

Moore, P.D. (ed) (1986), *The Collins Encyclopedia of Animal Ecology*, Collins, London.

Nelson, J.S. (1984), *Fishes of the World* (2nd edn), John Wiley and Sons, New York.

Ommanney, F. D. (1970), *The Fishes, Life Nature Library*, Time-Life Books.

Slater, P.J.B. (ed) (1986), *The Collins Encyclopedia of Animal Behaviour*, Collins, London.

Wheeler, A.C. (1969), *The Fishes of the British Isles and Northwest Europe*, Macmillan, London.

ACKNOWLEDGEMENTS

Picture credits

Key: *t* top. *b* bottom. *c* centre. *l* left. *r* right.
Abbreviations: A Ardea. AN Agence Nature. ANT Australasian Nature Transparencies. BCL Bruce Coleman Ltd. NHPA Natural History Photographic Agency. NSP Natural Science Photos. OSF Oxford Scientific Films. PEP Planet Earth Pictures. SAL Survival Anglia Ltd.

6 BCL/H. Reinhard. 8 OSF/Alastair Macewen. 9l BCL/J. Burton. 9r AN. 10 A. van den Nieuwenhuizen. 11 BCL/Jane Burton. 12 PEP/Ken Lucas. 15 A/V. Taylor. 16 OSF/G. Bernard. 18-19 OSF/G.I. Bernard. 20 BCL/M.P. Kahl. 21l A/K Fink. 21r PEP/B. Cocker. 22 AN. 23t D. Allison. 23b PEP/Ken Lucas. 24 PEP/P. Scoones. 25t PEP/Ken Lucas. 25b SAL/A. Root. 26-27t OSF/E.R. Degginger. 26-27b A/J Mason. 27 PEP/K. Lucas. 29 PEP/H. Voigtmann. 30 PEP/J. Lythgoe. 31 BCL/A. Power. 33 PEP/C. Roessler. 34 ANT/G. Schmida. 35 PEP/Dick Clarke. 38-39 PEP/G van Ryckerorsel. 39 OSF/David Thompson. 40t Leonard Lee Rue. 40c & b SAL/J. Foott. 41t NSP/G. Kinns & P. Ward. 41b BCL/L. Rue. 45 OSF/P. Parks. 46t OSF/P. Parks. 46b AN. 47 NHPA/Chaumeton-Bassot. 48 OSF/P. Parks. 50-51 A/P. Morris. 51t PEP/Ken Lucas. 52 PEP/Peter David. 54, 54-55, 55l, 55r BCL/J. Burton. 56l PEP/K. Lucas. 56r ANT/G. Schmida. 57t SAL/J. Root. 57b BCL/J. Simon. 60 PEP/J. Greenfield. 61 PEP/P. David. 63 SAL/J. Foot. 66 OSF/C. Roessler. 67t PEP/Alan Colclough. 67b OSF/R. Kuiter. 68-69 PEP/K. Amsler. 71tl BCL/J. Burton. 71tr OSF/R. Kuiter. 71br PEP/H. Jones. 72 PEP/P. Scoones. 73 PEP/D. Clarke. 76 OSF/G. Bernard. 77 ANT/G. Schmida. 82 PEP/K. Amsler. 83 PEP. 84-85 OSF/Z. Leszczynski. 85 PEP/G. Douwma. 86 Biofotos/H. Angel. 87 BCL/J. Burton. 88-89, 89 OSF/Z. Leszczynski. (Page 4 Ardea).

Artwork credits.

Key: *t* top. *b* bottom. *c* centre. *l* left. *r* right.
Abbreviations: DO Denys Ovenden. ML Mick Loates. NW Norman Weaver. OI Ltd Oxford Illustrators Ltd RL Richard Lewington. SD Simon Driver.

7SD. 8 Equinox Ltd. 9 OI Ltd. 10 Equinox Ltd. 12-13, 16-17 DO. 20 OI Ltd. 25 Equinox Ltd. 30 ML. 31, 32, 36-37 DO. 40, 42t ML. 42-43 DO. 44 ML. 49, 52, 53, 58-59 DO. 61 NW. 62 RL. 65, 70, 74, 77, 79 DO. 80 NW. 81, 85 DO. 86, 89 ML.